THE YOUNG

The Young Lions

1,000 Days of Training Under a Karate Legend
and the 100-Man Kumite

BY

JUDD REID

with Anton Cavka and Norm Schriever

THE YOUNG LIONS
An Epic Story of Perseverance, Chasing Your Dream and Never Giving Up

Copyright ©2016 by Judd Reid. All rights reserved.

Cover Design by Judd Reid

Cover Layout by Eclectic Cattle Productions, EclecticCattleProds.com

Interior Design & Layout by Jon J. Cardwell

DEDICATION

若獅子

In honour and memory, my best friend, Anton Cavka
This is for you, mate.
6 feet peakkkk,Tonnsa!

This book is dedicated to my teacher, Master Sosai Oyama. Osu

To my family, my rock, my mum: Kerry Rizzoli, and Peter (Rizza), Alex, Georgia and Marnie

To the Cavka family: Marjorie, Anton Senior, Jacqui, Mike and Nick

To my beautiful wife Mothana and my son Max, nothing can make a father more proud

To Norm Schriever, my brother, without you this book would not be possible

Uchi Deshi brothers: Nick Pettas, Yamakagi (Pink Panther), Karuda, Kato, Suzuki, Kato, Oshikiri, Komukai, Ishida, Ligo, Sandor, Mohammed, Ishiguro Senpai, Yameda Senpai and Hashimoto Senpai

Brunswick Dojo

In loving memory to my first teacher Ann Bradshaw. I miss you dearly Ann

Beckett and Trevor Frith

Elwood Dojo - Shihan Eddie Emin, Joy Emin, Trevor E and Billy

My Mentor Manny

Tiff K and Tiff's gorgeous mum

Nick Zaz, Tommy M, Ernie, Trifon, Gary Clarke, Duncan. Mark the Hammer, Joe Sayah

In loving memory Anton Vojic

My hero Wada Sensei, hope we can meet again one day soon

The 100 Man Fight crew: Mac, JR, Tommy Z, Naoki, Hangover Ben and Lewis

Emin

Duncan Cameron

Kosta

Kiley Baker

Tony W

Nick Murf

House of Pain - Nedda, Michael D, Costa, Glen, Dan, Steve Romic and Kym "Wolf Man"

Ronin Katz

DT Mohammad Bahrami - malloooooo

Vivien, Nick Kara. Hashbaaaasa

100manfight support team - Paul Phillips, Nick Beggs, Phil Jacobson, Steve, Kym, Francesco

RIP Daniel Fox

Darren Jordan

Jason Griffiths - blessed

Scot Powell - soldier!

Patrick Pinto

Justin Ward

Ishi Sensei

Jim Phillips

Todd Pantland, William and Vincent

Tim Hook

Dean Booth - 100 more camps to go!

Shohba, Josh, the parents and students from CKI

Travis (st), Cris and Jordy

Sugihara Soshi, Mizuguchi Kancho, Ishikawa Shihan, Minami Shihan

TABLE OF CONTENTS

若獅子

Foreword by Anton Cavka	xvii
Chapter 1: 100 Fights to Glory	1
Chapter 2: The Early Days	3
Chapter 3: Anne Bradshaw and the Brunswick Dojo	9
Chapter 4: The Turning Point	13
Chapter 5: Shihan Eddie and the St. Kilda Dojo	17
Chapter 6: Wada Sensei	21
Chapter 7: Manny, My Mentor	27
Chapter 8: First Love	29
Chapter 9: The God Hand	31
Chapter 10: My Quest to Become an *Uchi Deshi*	37
Chapter 11: Welcome to the 100-Man Fight	41
Chapter 12: Judd Reid, The Chalkie	45
Chapter 13: Black Belt Grading	49
Chapter 14: Sacrificing Everything for My Dream	51
Chapter 15 Enter The Dragon	55
Chapter 16: Meeting My Master	63
Chapter 17: *Hajime!* Starting the 100-Man Fight	65
Chapter 18: The Young Lions	69
Chapter 19: Baptism by Fire	77
Chapter 20: Hardships of Being a First-Year *Uchi Deshi*	85
Chapter 21: 100-Man *Kumite*, Fights 10 Through 30	91

Chapter 22: Life in the *Honbu*	93
Chapter 23: Classes with Sosai	109
Chapter 24: Fighting My Hero, Wada Sensei	113
Chapter 25: The Saddest Time	117
Chapter 26: 100-Man *Kumite,* Fights 30 Through 50	139
Chapter 27: The All Japan Open Weight Tournament	141
Chapter 28: The Japanese Way	145
Chapter 29: Moving Up the Ranks as a Young Lion	153
Chapter 30: Second-Year Promotion and Arrival of an Ally	157
Chapter 31: Elvis, Anime and Salarymen; Welcome to Tokyo	161
Chapter 32: Taking Classes in the *Honbu*	167
Chapter 33: 100-Man *Kumite,* Fights 51 Through 59	171
Chapter 34: A Thorn Among Roses	173
Chapter 35: Summer and Winter Camps	177
Chapter 36: Changes in the Cast	183
Chapter 37: Farewell to the Man They Called "Mokodomo"	187
Chapter 38: 100-Man *Kumite,* Fights 60 Through 70s	191
Chapter 39: Friendship, Rivalry and Cruelty in the Dojo	195
Chapter 40: Nick's Grading	205
Chapter 41: Ikebukuro and the *Yakuza*	209
Chapter 42: Suzuki and Me, Dueling it Out	213
Chapter 43: The Ranger Makes His Move	217
Chapter 44: The 100-Man *Kumite,* Fights 70 Through 90	221
Chapter 45: King of the World	223
Chapter 46: Nick's Turn	229

Chapter 47: Dinners with Sosai	233
Chapter 48: Getting in Trouble	239
Chapter 49: Brothers in Arms	243
Chapter 50: 100-Man *Kumite*, Fights 91 Through 99	247
Chapter 51: Graduation	249
Chapter 52: The Real Sosai Oyama	253
Chapter 53: 100-Man *Kumite* – My Final Fight	257
Afterword	261

若獅子

Photo Gallery	121
Glossary of Japanese Words	265

FOREWORD

若獅子

When I first got together with my mate, Judd, after he was fresh out of three years training in Japan as something called a Young Lion, we went golfing in our hometown of Melbourne. Judd was no longer the skinny kid I'd known when he'd left Australia 1,000 days earlier, but now had packed on 20 kg of solid steel to his frame. His smile and joking manner was the same, but everything else was different about him: he carried himself with an air of strength and confidence that was hard to define.

I asked him to explain the training he had just been through. He told me a little bit about the superhuman Kyokushin Karate training he'd been through, training under Master Sosai Mas Oyama, but remained characteristically humble. When I asked him to show me something that he'd learned, Judd looked around and then set his sights on a tree standing by the side of the fairway. He approached the tree and, to my amazement, unleashed a ferocious roundhouse kick to its trunk.

I heard a cracking sound and half expected it to be Judd's leg that had shattered, so my jaw dropped when I saw the tree trunk splinter, the crown starting to sag towards the ground.

Judd was apologetic, as he hadn't expected to break the tree trunk with one kick, and then went on golfing like nothing had happened. But I was in shock. "How can a human being do that?" I thought. "What the hell had they done to him in Japan for those 1,000 days?"

In 1990, a 19-year-old Australian kid named Judd Reid was hand picked by Kyokushin Karate founder Sosai Oyama to go to Japan and become one of his live-in students, or Young Lions. For 1,000 days, Sosai Oyama – a living legend they called the

"God Hand" – trained Reid and his other students under the most grueling and spartan conditions imaginable, pushing them way past the limits of human endurance.

I was always fascinated and awed by what Judd accomplished. The Young Lions were the elite of the elite of fight training, and Judd not only had to survive the physical tests, but acclimate to a completely foreign culture, and after those three years he was speaking Japanese fluently. But Mas Oyama wasn't just building great fighters, but men of great character, to go out into the world and spread the spirit of Kyokushin and make society better.

Three years later, Reid emerged as the first westerner to ever graduate as a Young Lion, setting him on a path as a professional fighter that would one day lead him to a World Championship and the ultimate challenge at the twilight of his career: the 100-man fight, or *kumite*.

It was something out of the movies: a secretive invitation-only event in Japan where you'd have to fight 100 black belts or experienced karate fighters in a row with no breaks. It's been described as doing a triathlon with people punching and kicking you the whole time. Moreover, Judd was already 40 years old when he was invited to attempt the 100-man *kumite* in 2010, which was an impossible feat even for younger fighters in their prime. In fact, only 18 fighters in history had completed the 100-man *kumite* before.

And to put it all on the line by taking on something like the 100-man *kumite* at the age of 40, after already becoming World Champion, was just insane. I mean, how many other endeavors can you say that only 18 other people did that? There have been 24 people in space throughout history, and thousands have climbed Mount Everest, but only 18 successfully finished the *kumite* before Judd?! That's crazy! It's like running a 3-minute mile!

I know all of this firsthand because I was Judd's best mate, living in Japan myself for 16 years, where I owned a very successful company that exported *The Fast and the Furious* type racecars around the world. I must admit that I lived an equally fast and furious lifestyle in Tokyo!

After a bout with cancer in 2010, I finally retired from that crazy lifestyle. At that time, Judd was training full force in Thailand for his upcoming 100-man *kumite*, so I thought it was a perfect time to start following him around with a camera crew to document the whole thing.

Judd fought in his 100-man *kumite* on October 22, 2011 in Osaka, Japan, and we got the whole thing on film in the documentary, *Journey to The 100-Man Fight*. It was so warmly received by fight fans and karate enthusiasts around the world that we were urged to write a book – the story of Judd's life.

So over a few months in Thailand, Cambodia and Australia, we sat down over a thousand coffees (and a few beers) and finally committed Judd's story to the page: his childhood, detailed journey through Mas Oyama's legendary Young Lions program as a youth and, finally, his attempt to be only the 19th person in history to complete the 100-Man Fight.

I hope you love the result, and I can tell you that he poured himself into the book just like he goes at training – full on.

Sincerely,
Anton Cavka

P.S. In case you ever want to visit Japan, I'd say that the spring is a perfect time to go, because it's cherry blossom season. Their obsession with youth and perfection means that thousands of people travel around the countryside every year, trying to find the one perfect blossom.

The symbolism of it all is everything the Japanese are about, as they say that cherry blossoms are a metaphor for life:

So beautiful,
yet so very short.

若獅子

Tragically, Anton passed away in Phnom Penh, Cambodia before he could see this book finished. This story is dedicated to his memory.

若獅子

CHAPTER 1
100 FIGHTS TO GLORY

若獅子

By the time I got to my 62nd fight in a row that afternoon in Osaka, my game plan really started falling apart. I had trained like a man possessed for this 100-man *kumite* for four months straight in the oppressive heat of Asia, reaching the highest pinnacle of fitness of any time in my life. I guess I'd been training for this very moment since the day I first discovered karate, but still, I was wearing down, starting to absorb my opponent's powerful punches and kicks instead of blocking them all, like I had with my first 60 opponents. The cramping in my legs was a tightening vice, and I felt like I had a 200-pound (91 kg) log on my shoulders like the one I'd used in training.

But far worse than the physical punishment I was taking was the incredible loneliness I felt out on the mat, in spite of the couple of hundred people watching. Everyone's eyes were trained on me, and I knew they were all cheering for me to continue on, but I felt completely alone and defenseless. It was like I was tied to a tree in the desert and waiting for my demise. That was something I had anticipated – and couldn't train for.

The scariest part was that during the last few fights, I noticed my focus going in and out. My mind had drifted, and small cracks had started to appear in the strong mindset that I'd had only five minutes before. What the hell was happening to me? I'd gone from an invincible warrior to feeling vulnerable and weak. It was a terrible feeling, and I had to snap out of it quickly – otherwise it would be game-over for sure. This was my toughest hour, the most difficult moment I'd ever experienced in my entire decades-long fighting career.

I still had 38 fights left. That meant 38 fresh opponents – all black belts, and all instructed to come out and smash me. Heading back to my corner, looking up and trying to gather some strength, some will, my Japanese master Sosai Mas Oyama's words were ringing in my head. *"Yareba dekiru.* If you try, you can do it. *Kare wa kami sama janai yo. Kare mo ningen dayo.* Your opponent is not a god. He is human too. *Gambarre!* Fight on!"

I could tell that my punches and kicks were nowhere near as effective as they'd been five fights ago. Seeing my fatigue set in, my opponents were growing more emboldened, attacking my legs with heavy kicks, punches into my liver, kidneys and sides that were surely causing internal bleeding. I was starting to take a lot of damage unnecessarily. I had to snap out of this real quick or I wouldn't make it through 100 fights. Everything was on the line. "Concentrate, Judd," my mind screamed, rattling me back to focus. "Get it together! *Osu!*"

I had to choose my strikes carefully to conserve energy, but still finish my opponents as quickly as possible. I set him up with a few hooks to his body so his hands dropped just slightly, then I unleashed a high axe kick aimed at his head, but missed by less than an inch.

My legs were numb, my whole body was in agony, and my vision was blurry. Even my mind had started to give up on me, but I blocked out the pain and I refused to give in. I was fighting on heart alone, and that's all I had left.

I was going into battle with 100 accomplished karate fighters in a row, to become one of only 20 human beings ever to achieve that feat, and the oldest fighter to finish the Japanese *kumite*. I was going to get through this, no matter what – or die trying.

I sprang forward and unleashed a straight punch with all my might, trying not just to hit my opponent's chest, but to go right through it, roaring *kiai!* as loud as a lion.

CHAPTER 2
THE EARLY DAYS

若獅子

"As you think, so shall you become." –Bruce Lee

My father was never around when I grew up in Australia, starting from an early age. He stopped coming around when I was about nine. My mother was very young when I was born, and she had to leave her apprenticeship. My sister, Marnie, came seven years later, and my father was only with my mum until about two years after Marnie was born.

I think my mum and dad loved each other in the beginning, when they bought their own house in St. Albans and tried to live the family life. My father worked in the Courage Brewery, which probably wasn't the best job, as he was often drunk. He even had his own room in the house that was built like a saloon, complete with a full bar and swinging doors. The booze was free for workers at the CUB, so he would invite his friends over, including my dad's friend David, and they would see who could drink until they passed out. These days, some people would say he was an alcoholic.

My mum and dad fought a lot around that time, and eventually my mum couldn't take it anymore, so she took us kids and left. After that, my father only made sporadic visits to see me. He was basically not around for the rest of my childhood. My mum and dad argued a lot in the lead-up to this, but of course as a kid I wished they'd stayed together. Marnie was too young to really understand. My mum never actually sat us down and said that dad was gone forever, but that was how it turned out. For all intents and purposes my mum, Kerry, was left to raise two kids on her own. St. Albans was a rough area of

Melbourne in those days. It was a run-down, low socioeconomic area with all the usual problems that come with it. There were a lot of delinquent kids hanging around with not much to do, and I was getting into a lot of fights. Looking back, I had a real chip on my shoulder – probably because of what was happening at home. I guess, like most kids in broken homes, I felt abandoned with my dad not being there, so I put up a wall straight away. Although I never set out to start fights, I was never one to back down from an insult or a challenge, either. I was a small, skinny kid and an easy target. On my way home from school or walking through the neighborhood, it was plenty common for three kids to pick on me. These days they would call what happened to me bullying, but in those days in St. Albans, it was just the way life was. I dealt with it as best I could.

Just before I started Grade Five, we moved to a more middle-class, leafier suburb called Essendon. I enrolled at St. Therese's Catholic School but wasn't the brightest kid, having moved from Stevensville Primary School, so I struggled with schoolwork from the start. Stevensville wasn't exactly the epitome of higher learning in those days, as education wasn't at the forefront of the minds of the blue-collar workers who lived in St. Albans. I was at SPS from prep school 'til Grade 4, and then at STCS for two years.

When I was 11, the whole family picked up to travel around Europe. My mum, being only 27 at the time, wanted to experience life overseas, and so we travelled around France, Belgium, Amsterdam and Ireland before finally settling in Earl's Court in London. Earl's Court was right in the middle of the city, and it was a big change from Australia. The housing was mostly three-story cream-colored terraced buildings, and in those days it was a pretty run-down area. But I've got to say, with all the people and action going on, it was sparking with excitement, and there was a real adventurous vibe to it. My mum worked in a local pub. We lived in a run-down basement townhouse whose former tenant was engaged in the world's oldest profession, so when we first moved in men sometimes knocked on the door asking for her whereabouts. Whenever there was a knock, my mum would always rush to the door to shield innocent me from the reality of the situation.

Marnie and I went to a local public school just up the road from where we lived. The school was so multicultural that I was the one of the only white kids there. Most of the kids were Pakistani, Indian, South American, African and Asian. I really loved school there. It was fun, exciting and sport was a big part of the curriculum so I got to play soccer – the national sport of the UK. Earl's Court was a great time. The best part was that they served us food at both recess and lunch, and we could eat as much as we wanted. London wasn't exactly a cheap place to live and Mum didn't have a high-paying job, so the free food at school was a real bonus. I also remember the food was really good compared to my mum's vegemite and jam sandwiches.

I was always an active kid playing footy, cricket and other athletics like any normal Aussie kid. In the UK I was captain of the cricket team, and reasonably adept at most sports I tried. In those days there were no computers, smartphones or iPads like kids have now, so sport was my life.

In Earl's Court there was a park nearby, enclosed by a 10-foot-tall wrought iron fence that required a key to enter. I spent most of my time there playing sports, and one day I saw four Asian teenagers doing acrobatics and backflips there. I don't know what sort of martial art they were doing, but it completely blew me away. I'd never even seen a martial arts movie before, and I was completely enthralled. They were doing flashy kicks that I'd never seen before, and I was totally captivated by what they could do with their bodies. They saw me watching, wide-eyed, so were nice enough to call me over and teach me how to do a basic backflip. To me, they were real-life ninjas.

Mum intended to live in Earl's Court for a long time, but just after I turned 12 my grandmother became ill, so we returned to Australia. We moved to Moonee Ponds near Essendon and I was enrolled at the Moonee Ponds Central

School. My best mate at the time was a kid just as small as me named Nick Murphy. He was thin and wiry but tenacious, and had a great spirit and zest for life. We both loved new adventures and had no fear, so immediately became best mates. Our school was down near the Moonee Valley Race Course and I lived about two miles away. We used to ride our bikes to and from school every day, and I found myself getting into even more fights with the local kids, both at school and in the streets. I had picked up a bit of an English accent in London, which didn't help, and looking back, my anger over my dad leaving us had quite an impact on me.

I had a lot of fire in my belly in those early days. I remember it was just before I started karate when I got jumped by a half a dozen kids at a park near my home. The kids surrounded my bike and stopped me, and for no reason at all they started punching into me. I was getting hit in the face and the back of the head, and then they ran off. It probably only lasted about 30 seconds, and they didn't really hurt me physically, but the whole incident ripped into me emotionally. I remember riding home furiously, crying with adrenaline and anger. I made myself a Monkey Magic Stick – cutting off a broomstick and painting it black with gold stripes so it looked like the sticks they used in the popular kids martial arts TV series. When I got home, I grabbed the stick and rode straight back to the park looking for those kids, shaking with rage, but they were no longer there. I thought I could use the stick and do my monkey magic moves on them, though I probably would have just knocked myself on the head instead!

I remember when kids started fights with me, I'd yell out to Nick, "Hey Nick, hold my watch!" and throw him my wristwatch so I could fight without having to tell my mum how another one got smashed. Nick caught a lot of my watches in those days. The reasons were never really that clear why we fought, but it was a different time, and although people these days say violence is much more prevalent now, they are kidding themselves.

The Early Days

While I was still 12 years old, Mum took me to see three Bruce Lee movies at the old drive-in theatre in Coburg. Normally my mum would take Marnie and me to see horror movies like The Amityville Horror, The Exorcist, The Shining and Friday the 13th (even though Marnie was only about four at the time!), as my mum was a huge horror fan. This was a regular thing for us, and always in our old, beat-up Volkswagen at the last of Melbourne's drive-ins. One weekend, my mum and I were flicking through the paper, seeing what was showing at the drive-in, and I put my little foot down and said, "Mum, no more horror movies, please." I saw a movie ad of some Asian guy doing a flying side kick and said, "We're going to see that!"

I remember the movies: Fist of Fury, The Big Boss and The Way of The Dragon, the last one with Bruce Lee and Chuck Norris fighting in their famous scene in the Coliseum. After watching those movies, I was completely and totally hooked.

At that age, I thought Bruce Lee wasn't acting but telling a real story, so when Bruce Lee gets shot and dies in the very last scene of Fist of Fury, I was devastated. I thought they'd just killed my hero. Only after did I see the other two movies and realize that, thank god, Bruce is still alive.

I remember feeling I was on the edge of my seat when he was fighting Chuck Norris in the famous Coliseum scene, and although he looked like he would lose, he eventually won, killing Chuck Norris. I wanted to be Bruce Lee. He was small like me, but fearless and tough. He could take on anyone.

I immediately bought a Bruce Lee poster and hung it in my bedroom. I told my mum I wanted to do karate – the only martial art really available in those days – so she looked in the Yellow Pages and found a school in nearby Brunswick. Just by pure luck, it was a Kyokushin Karate school. I had no idea this childhood decision would shape my life forever.

I started doing karate at the age of 12, thanks to a Bruce Lee triple-feature and my desire to stand up to the bullies in the neighborhood. There are certainly a lot of martial arts schools around the world that can thank Bruce for the spread of martial arts and the success of their businesses.

When my mum first drove me to the karate school in Brunswick, I loved it immediately. It was very intense, with lots of loud screaming, or kias, when the students performed attacking moves. There was also a lot of punching, kicking, push-ups, sit-ups, and – best of all – discipline. The teacher walked around with a stick, and if you were sloppy, not paying attention or not giving 100%, you were hit with this shinai, a Japanese stick made out of bamboo. I didn't mind it, but you sure couldn't do that these days!

My mum was my rock. She was always very supportive, whether I was playing cricket, football or golf, and always encouraging me. She really encouraged me when I first starting doing karate because my grades improved immediately. Karate teaches you discipline, perseverance and full focus on the task at hand, so my training rubbed off on my schoolwork.

My mum drove me to the Brunswick school and picked me up whenever she could. She was a single mum in those days, working a lot of shifts as a nurse at Melbourne Pathology in Essendon, sacrificing a lot to support my sister and me. There must have been some tough times for my mum and I can honestly say that I owe her everything; but once karate was in my life, it would never leave, roaring *kiai!* as loud as a lion.

CHAPTER 3
ANNE BRADSHAW
AND THE BRUNSWICK DOJO

若獅子

My first karate school was at the Brunswick Town Hall, and my first teacher was Anne Bradshaw, who worked under Shihan Eddie Emin – a pioneer of Kyokushin Karate in Australia who was running four schools under his main school in St. Kilda.

Anne Bradshaw was a robust, red-haired woman in her mid-20s from Wales; she was a very nice person with a strong Welsh accent. Her strength and technique were fantastic, and she was certainly my first inspiration in karate. Anne was very positive, and all the students loved her. She made a terrific first instructor because she was very strict on technique, and everything had to be sharp and quick.

Anne was as serious about her karate technique as she was a lovely person. For such large lady, her kicking ability was so fast and her emphasis was always speed, in and out, moving around, and she looked like something out of the movies. Anne inspired us to work hard in class. There were probably about 10 to 15 students who were taught twice a week on Tuesday and Thursday, a mixture of adults and kids, and I was one of the youngest at age 12. We trained on hardwood floors at the Brunswick Town Hall, and we'd always end up with blisters and hurting ourselves; but that was all a part the process of building character and not stopping for anything.

Anne had previously won the Wales Championship, and I saw her fight in the Victorian Titles in 1984 where she won the open weight women's division. At that same Victorian Title, I remember seeing a young guy of about 18 years old fighting in the adult lightweight division, and he knocked out every one of the three fighters he fought. That left a lasting impression, because not only had I just started to do karate, but he was just incredible and explosive to watch. Fifteen years later, I met him by chance and found out his name was Michael Dugina, and we became very good friends.

Anne was my first inspiration as a young kid. She was tough on us, but also offered plenty of encouragement and words to motivate us. Looking back at it now, I'm glad that she was so strict on technique and discipline. As I mentioned, I still was a bit of a wild child and had a chip on my shoulder, but sure enough, thanks to Anne and the structure I learned through martial arts, my attitude changed forever.

For me, martial arts weren't like other sports that were simply about physical contact, skill and competition. Karate was more than that. You were in a *gi* (karate uniform), there were many traditions and a lot of etiquette to follow, and you were learning something that the average person was not. Not only that, but you were learning a sport that had meaning, as you could use the art of karate to defend yourself from the bullies of the world. Perhaps one day you could even use your skills to protect your family and friends from bad guys. It was mystical, it was becoming popular in the movies – even some more mainstream movies – and it had me hooked.

The kids at school and in the neighborhood were leaving me alone now, too. Martial arts are a special sport that instills confidence you exude in your daily life, and this reflects on how other people treat you. With confidence, you gain respect. Even just looking other kids in the eye and speaking clearly tells them you are not afraid, and they can sense this.

Karate was unlike boxing, which was a more mainstream. Kyokushin Karate was a martial art that taught you everything from fighting skills to fitness, flexibility to discipline, and a way of thinking that the average person didn't understand. I was obsessed – too much for a 12-year-old, really, but it's better to be obsessed with a sport than a vice. I improved quickly and within a couple of years the kids at school were referring to me as the "real-life Karate Kid." I thought this was amusing at the time, but it wasn't a bad reputation to have. As teenagers, everyone had posters up on their walls. Some had rock bands, other famous actors, sports stars or models. I had Bruce Lee, and later on, Sosai Oyama, the living legend in Japan who would change the course of my life and become like a father to me.

CHAPTER 4
THE TURNING POINT

若獅子

Growing up, I really resented my dad because he rarely visited us. When I got back from the UK, I used to see my dad about every two weeks, then that drifted to about once a month, but by age 14 he completely disappeared, which built up a lot of hurt and anger inside of me.

Looking back, sport was my release. I liked to play any sport, really, and before I got hooked on karate my passion was golf. I started playing golf at 13 and without bragging you could say I was naturally gifted, playing off a 14 handicap at the age of 14. I played pennant golf on the weekend, and my part-time job was to drive the tractor across the driving range, picking up golf balls that the paying public was hitting.

At the age of 14 I was also playing Australian rules football, and my coach was Peter Rizzoli. He was a big strong guy with a moustache, someone who was always very positive and inspiring, and to me he looked like an Iron Man. Ironically, my mum met Peter because I played football, and they developed a relationship. They got married when I was about 15 and have been together ever since, having two daughters, Alex and Georgia, who are only three years apart but more than 22 years younger than me. Even though there was a male in the house for a lot of my youth, there was never really one solid father figure until my football coach, Peter, and my mother got married, and I couldn't have been happier for my mum to settle down. I really looked up to him, and he inspired me as an athlete – always telling me to grit your teeth, go hard at the ball, and give it your best. He is a great guy, and even a good mate, and I still always call him Rizza.

At that stage I was really into footy and golf, so I had very little time for much else. Without someone like Anne I would probably not have continued in martial arts. There was no picture of Kyokushin Karate founder Sosai Mas Oyama at the front of the class and no mention of him. To be honest, I only knew I was doing karate under Anne and I loved it. Looking back, I doubt I would have even been able to pronounce the word *Kyokushin*.

I trained at the Brunswick Town Hall for two and a half years, until it closed because Anne had to stop teaching due to personal reasons. I was about 15 years old when the dojo closed down, and I remember being very saddened and distressed by this.

At that time, I was also playing golf seriously. I even had a part-time job working at Essendon Golf Course scooping up balls on the driving range in one of those caged golf tractors. I loved this job, even though now and again some balls would go flying into the cage. But I would just laugh it off, because it was usually hit by one of the guys I worked for. We had a lot of fun, and on the weekends I would play pennant golf representing the club, playing against adults off a handicap of 14. One Christmas we went up to Queensland for a holiday, and halfway through the holiday I caught a train back to Melbourne to play in a big golf tournament. My mum and Rizza thought I was a bit obsessed with this, but encouraged me all the way. I stayed at Nic's house and I played in the golf tournament that weekend. I did pretty well and I finished in the top 15 out of about 150 people. My golf teacher (and boss) was very proud of me.

After the Christmas holiday, school started but I had no dojo to train at. About the time the Brunswick dojo closed down, we moved from Essendon to Strathmore – a couple of suburbs down – and my mum told me I needed to choose one sport. Since the Brunswick school closed down, the nearest Kyokushin dojo was in St. Kilda, which was on the other side of town. I'd have to catch two trains and a bus, taking over two hours to get there. The trains were hopeless back then, forever late and cancelled all the time. I asked my mum if I could join that karate school, and she said yes. She was a bit worried because I was so young, but I said I'd be all right. In my bag I carried a pair of nunchucks, schoolbooks, a diary and my karate uniform. Over time, only the karate uniform and diary would remain.

CHAPTER 5
SHIHAN EDDIE
AND THE ST. KILDA DOJO

若獅子

"Water can support a ship and water can also sink a ship."
–Old Chinese proverb

Initially, Shihan Eddie's dojo was the St. Kilda Town Hall. But after a few months we moved to a new location in nearby Tennyson Street, Elwood that housed 10 squash courts and a dojo out the back. As students, we helped build the dojo, and the Elwood dojo was world class with a fantastic atmosphere. Shihan Eddie and the students who attended were super keen on making it a first class dojo. Amongst others, we had Tommy McMahon, who went on to open his own dojo; Mark "Hammer" Castagnini, who went on to become a professional kickboxer and commentator and eventually open a gym; and Manny, who loved the spiritual side of martial arts and all things Japanese.

Shihan Eddie was the actual owner of the school and, in technical terminology, was branch chief for Melbourne. The branch chief is the person in control of that region, and at that time there were about six Kyokushin Karate branch chiefs – one in each state of Australia – charged with the responsibility to uphold the high standards of Kyokushin, as well as organize and hold tournaments. To be a branch chief you had to be chosen by Kyokushin Karate founder Sosai Mas Oyama, and that honor made you an ambassador of the sport. Even in Japan, there would have been only about 30 branch chiefs in those days, and only about 60 in the world. So in those days,

Australia's contingent outside of Japan was considered large. Kyokushin also had a large presence in America, Brazil, England and Africa. In all, it was estimated there were already up to 10 million members. It was mandated that $25 of every Kyokushin membership was supposed to kick back to the Honbu, or home dojo, in Tokyo, but even to this day it's never been verified whether that actually happened. The contributions were supposed to allow founder Sosai Oyama to run the organization and hold national and world tournaments with 250 competitors, and probably as many coaches, officials and invited guests, all of whom had their airfares and hotels paid for. That probably added up to around a couple of million dollars – a lot of money in those days.

Shihan Eddie was quite a character, with long black hair, a long Fu Manchu style moustache and a goatee beard. He always reminded us students of a Chinese kung fu master out of the movies. He was always full of energy and full of beans, despite the fact that he was already 50 years old and had a bad knee, which made him walk with a limp. To this day he has never changed – he's almost ageless. Shihan Eddie spoke in a loud voice in an authoritative way, and he was equally strong and intimidating. He had the full attention of us youngsters and taught us incredible discipline. He was the one who always carried a shinai – a stick made of bamboo – and if we did anything wrong, whether displaying poor technique, poor concentration, bad focus, talking in class or being fidgety, he wouldn't hesitate to smack you over the forearm, legs or stomach to get you back in line. It would sting a little and occasionally leave a mark, but never to the point that it would cause any permanent or serious damage – just enough to make you concentrate in class and do the right thing next time.

Shihan Eddie was incredibly strict on form, and the techniques all had to be executed perfectly. He did a lot of basics, which gave us all a great foundation, and nothing was allowed to be sloppy or out of place. He initially ran his classes out of the St. Kilda Town Hall and had about 30 students – a mixture of adults and kids. We began building the dojo at the back of the Elwood squash courts within three months of my start, on a parcel of spare land behind the squash courts. Until it was completed, we trained right in the squash courts, but within six months the dojo was complete with a wooden floor about 20 by 35 feet, a picture of Sosai Oyama at the front, and an Australian and a Japanese flag on either side of the picture.

I started to learn the history of Sosai Oyama when I was doing my gradings with Shihan Eddie, including the history of Kyokushin, Sosai Mas Oyama and even the Japanese terminology for the different karate techniques. At 12 I started as a white belt. Under Anne I went from white to blue to yellow to green over a two-year period. Then, under Shihan Eddie, I went from green to brown, and finally achieving my black belt at the age of 17-and-a-half, after more than five years of training.

Shihan Eddie's classes went for at least two hours, and at that stage I really stepped up my training. I attended Monday, Wednesday, Thursday, Friday and even Saturday classes – which were for the senior brown belts and above, with an emphasis on fighting.

Shihan Eddie was a great talker, and at the end of the class he would make everyone sit in the seiza position (basically, kneeling with your legs tucked under you), and he would talk about philosophical things in life that sometimes went from 10 minutes up to an hour while our legs were going numb. He would often say mokuso, which would mean you close your eyes to concentrate, and he would have us imagine we were standing under a waterfall or at the beach, and he would wax poetic about his ideas about of life. His subject matter would cover everything from conducting yourself in public, to avoiding or dealing with thugs on the street, to doing well at school, and doing the right thing by your friends and family. I always took something away from Shihan Eddie's talks.

Shihan Eddie was perhaps the most passionate person I've ever encountered in karate. He was also a taxi driver, owning two taxis and driving around working outside of his school hours. Once his dojo was built, his school grew bigger and bigger, and from 30 students at the St. Kilda Town Hall his student numbers had tripled to more than 100 by the time I was a black belt.

CHAPTER 6
WADA SENSEI

若獅子

"The great mistake is to anticipate the outcome of the engagement; you ought not to be thinking of whether it ends in victory or defeat. Let nature take its course, and your tools will strike at the right moment."
–Bruce Lee

The first time I met Wada Sensei was a couple of weeks after I started training at the St. Kilda Town Hall in 1987. I had moved there from the Brunswick school at almost exactly the same time Wada had arrived from Japan. He was a former uchi deshi, or live-in student, of Sosai Oyama. He was about 22 or 23, and as with all uchi deshi, Sosai Oyama used to send them around the world to spread the word of Kyokushin for a year or more. Wada Sensei was a graduate of the Young Lions program in Japan, essentially uchi deshi who lived and trained intensely for 1,000 days straight, a course that thousands of candidates applied for each year, but only a handful got accepted. And now his assignment was to come to Australia and teach us for a year. I was captivated.

Wada Sensei spoke little English in the beginning, and even after a year still only spoke a few basic words and phrases. Watching him train, I was blown away, always left thinking, "Who is this superhero?" He could do freaky kicks, with an uncanny ability to demonstrate and step us through each kick while holding his leg in the air for a long time. He could hold his leg straight up in the air and pivot around for minutes at a time as he explained how each technique worked. He was about 165 pounds (75 kg), only 5'8", but pure muscle. He was an incredible technician with perfect form. I was amazed, and the rest of the school was in awe of him, too.

The fact that Wada couldn't speak English didn't matter, as everything was demonstrated by his actions. From the beginning, even under Anne Bradshaw, instructions were given in Japanese, so listening to Wada Sensei and learning was familiar and easy.

After we got to know him, a lot of us students were so inspired that we came to the dojo up to two hours before class to hang out with him. My fellow students Tommy, Nick, Trifon, Anton and I, we would just hang around and imitate him. He would do weight training, some hitting and kicking of the bag, stretching, and we would just shadow him to copy his every move. He was even nice enough to take the time to correct us, and quickly he had his own fan club of young Aussie wannabe karate kids.

Wada Sensei became my hero, even more than Bruce Lee. I would study on the train. My grades had actually improved a lot, and my mum and Peter were happy that karate was making a big difference in my schooling. After school, I would all-out sprint to the train station as soon as the final bell had rung, so I could get to the dojo around 5:30 PM and start training immediately.

I think some of the kids at school thought I was a bit over the top because I wouldn't join in any of the games they were playing. I preferred to practice the techniques I learnt the night before, trying to get them 100% right. As far as I was concerned, any kind of training was good, and Wada Sensei could see that I was keen and gave my absolute best every time.

Now that I'd finished with golf, my full attention was on karate training. I remember coming home after training and catching the connecting trains, sometimes getting home as late as 11:30 PM. I would heat up the food my mum had left in the oven, drink as much milk as I could, and then every night before going to sleep I would do dips 'til I couldn't do anymore. It's fair to say that I was completely obsessed.

I knew Wada Sensei was an uchi deshi of Sosai Oyama, and

Sosai had sent him out to teach at our dojo. It was normal for the uchi deshi to be sent overseas after graduating, for up to three years after serving as Sosai's personal live-in student. The idea was to spread Kyokushin Karate worldwide, and uchi deshi were the most respected because they were direct students of the master, Sosai Oyama. Who else could be better to spread this amazing art?

It was on one of those long train rides back home that the idea popped into my head that would change my life. "I want to go to Japan and be an uchi deshi. I want to be like Wada Sensei and do exactly what he did." Soon it became all I thought about. Sitting on the train at night, staring out the window into the darkness, I imagined myself living and training in Japan. That was my sole vision and dream. I would scribble in my diary as the train shook from side to side, trying to steady my hand so the writing would be legible: "I am going to Japan. I will be an uchi deshi of Sosai Oyama." I did this every night I came back from training. I was 100% dedicated to getting there.

I started to dislike school because I knew karate was my destiny, so I started missing classes. I began leaving school around 1 PM so I could get into the dojo early and join the Wada fan club. I would write forged notes, signing my mum's signature, saying, "Judd is sick, and sorry he has been missing school." My grades suffered, but I didn't care. I had a plan – a pretty crazy ambition, when I think about it now. How was I, some skinny kid from a small dojo in Australia, going to go to Japan and become one of the great Sosai Oyama's Young Lions?

I would hang around and watch, imitating Wada Sensei's every move. Some of the kids lived close by, so it was easy for them to get there by 3:30. Tommy was one of them. We tried not to get in the way as we mimicked every punch, kick, stretch and even breath Wada Sensei took. He could see we were eager, so he let us join his training, and that was like winning the lottery for me; I was so happy. He took us underneath his wing, and we would train for about two hours, then he would sometime take us for a bite to eat. He was such a nice guy, but I'm sure sometimes he thought, "Don't these kids ever give up?!"

I remember Tommy and I went to a Japanese restaurant with Wada Sensei once. Of course we couldn't use chopsticks properly but, boy, Wada Sensei was like an eating machine.

He held the rice bowl up to his mouth and shoveled that rice down so fast you had to see it to believe it. Tommy and I couldn't stop laughing. We knew it was rude to laugh, but we couldn't help it; we were in tears. I don't think he noticed, or else he just didn't care. He was on a mission to smash that bowl of rice down the same way he would train in class, full steam ahead, like the Terminator.

By now my brain was totally focused on karate alone. Instead of studying school assignments on the train to the dojo, I would study the Japanese alphabet hiragana and katakana instead. I was determined to be able to write Japanese. Later on, this proved to be a huge asset. In my schoolbook or diary I would write every day: "One day I will be an uchi deshi," and what my weaknesses were, and what I needed to improve upon. I would write this on the train every day as others went to and from work and the stations blurred by. To 'this day I have this diary. It's very dear to me, and I smile to myself saying, "See? If you want something bad enough, you can succeed."

I was getting stronger every day, but halfway through Year 11, the school principal called my mum into the school and asked if I was OK. They thought I was very sick, since I had so many absences. When I got home, my mum stood in my bedroom with a piece of paper in her hand. On the paper was her name, written a number of times. She was holding the evidence that I'd forged her signature (and become quite good at it). She told me that the principal had said I was in big, big trouble.

The next day, early in the morning, my mum held my hand tight and marched me straight to the principal's office. As you can imagine, it is extremely embarrassing being dragged into school with your mum holding your hand, an angry look on her face, and saying to me, "Don't you dare let go of my hand."

It wasn't looking good. The principal thought I was really sick and had been concerned about me, but when the truth came out, he wasn't impressed. He said, "Judd, you might as well quit this year, as there is no way you can pass."

In my heart I was relieved, thinking, "Great, I can go straight back to training!"

My mum and Rizza were furious. They said, "What are you thinking, forging my signature, lying about going to school?" My mum said I was grounded and not allowed out of the house.

I was devastated. I locked myself in my room and refused to come out except for food. I didn't say a word to anyone in the house. I think it went on like this for about two weeks before my mum said, "Right, you'll get a part-time job, and you can go back to training." I was rapt. I worked at Pizza Hut as a dishwasher, and then went straight to the dojo. Life was great.

I decided to go full steam ahead in karate because of Wada Sensei. I couldn't see myself going to university, couldn't see myself working, nothing like that. Wada Sensei inspired me to train harder, and I tried to be like him. As a young kid, you are very impressionable, and he was my hero at the time. My family knew from the time I was 16 or 17 that I wanted to go to Japan. I talked so much about karate I bet I did their heads in. They probably didn't think I would actually ever do it, but when they found out that Wada Sensei had made a recommendation on my behalf, they realized it might be realistic.

As a karateka, I never really considered the fact that I might get injured. You just have to train hard and leave the doubts out of your mind. If you have no doubts, you have the confidence to go out and fight the best you can. I enjoyed competition fighting. I loved to fight, to test my abilities. I loved the adrenaline it gave me, and the whole atmosphere of a tournament. In the beginning I loved the learning aspect of everything, walking away exhausted but exhilarated, dragging your feet out of the dojo but having learned something new. Fresh blood pumping through your veins, but having gotten fitter and stronger, and having learned something. If you have a tournament coming up and you are fit and strong, it makes things so much more enjoyable.

We used to have summer and winter training camps, and Shihan Eddie would bring films such as The Strongest Karate, which showed Sosai Oyama wrestling bulls, doing demonstrations and giving speeches, and he seemed such a strong powerful person. He was God to me. In front of the class there was a picture of him, and at the start of every class we would bow to Sosai, and at the end we would read the dojo kun, or Kyokushin Oath. It instilled a sense of respect and belief, and as far as I was concerned we were swearing allegiance to him. He was a superhuman being, the ultimate authority on teaching karate, on living your life and knowing how to live life correctly. Not all the students believed this as strongly as me, but we all knew that Kyokushin changed people for the better.

I even had a picture of Sosai Oyama in my bedroom, above my bed on the other side of Bruce Lee, which made my room look like a dojo. Because Sosai Oyama was there in my room, I bowed and said "osu" when I entered my room. My mum was super happy because I kept my room spotlessly clean like the dojo, and I also had my karate gi and belt folded very nicely in the cupboard or on a chair. I remember some other students, even higher grades, throwing their belts and karate gis on the ground in the change rooms after training and thinking, "How could you do that?"

Karate was my religion, Wada Sensei my teacher and Sosai Oyama my god – and I was fast becoming the most devout follower.

CHAPTER 7
MANNY, MY MENTOR

若獅子

"Remember that you must always have a deep regard for courtesy, and you must be respectful and obedient toward your seniors."
— Gichin Funakoshi

I first met Manny at St. Kilda Town Hall. Manny Tsuvolcluu was one of about 32 students training there at the time. He was a fireman, married, had a small child, and lived not far from the dojo. Manny also was as passionate about karate as I was. He took me under his wing when I started at the Elwood dojo, and we got along very well. I was training five times a week, and the fact that I trained in the Friday night class and also wanted to train with the Saturday senior class the following morning would have been almost impossible for me if not for him. Manny offered to let me to stay with him on Friday nights, and sometimes on Saturdays, to save me the trip back to my mum's place in Strathmore. His wife always made us a huge bowl of pasta on Fridays after training, so we would have enough energy for the senior session the next day.

Manny was just as obsessed with karate as I was, and he encouraged me to study the Japanese alphabets *hiragana* and *katakana*. He loved Japanese culture and martial arts. He lived in nearby Balaclava at the time, and his house was full of Japanese artifacts. He had a full Japanese garden, a Japanese pond, stone paths, and bonsai trees behind his house. Inside, he had a *makiwara* set up – a post with some padding, which you would punch to condition your hands – as well as a big punching bag for training.

Manny was a green belt, like me, and we got along very

well – good mates, even though he was 32 and I was just 15. He would read karate magazines and encouraged me to do the same. He even gave me a karate book called *The Essence of Karate* by Gichin Funakoshi, the founder of Shotokan karate and one of Sosai Oyama's first teachers.

Gichin Funakoshi was a legendary figure and Shotokan karate was the most popular style of early Japanese karate, with millions of practitioners worldwide. In *The Essence of Karate*, Funakoshi explains the philosophical and spiritual underpinnings of karate and includes memories of his own training, as well as recollections of other karate masters and the history of the martial arts. He also discusses the importance of winning without fighting, and the reason why many great martial artists improve with age. I didn't fully appreciate the meaning of the book at the time, but came to realize later on that it was very closely aligned with the way Manny thought about his own karate. Where I thought karate training was for tournaments and fighting, Manny thought it was more about fitness, mastering technique, discipline, and inner peace.

Manny and I got along very well and both adored Wada Sensei and our training, and all we talked about was karate. His wife's name was Beth, and she was super cool and loved what we did. Manny lived a clean life. He didn't drink, and was a very positive person. He was kind of heart, and trained his guts out, and the timing of us meeting and then training at the Elwood school was a lucky turn of fate, and a golden time in my youth.

Manny was my mentor during these years. I sometimes even stayed overnight at the fire station when he was on call, though I remember not wanting to leave my sleeping quarters for fear of setting off an alarm.

My mum often said that young kids could go astray, so she loved Manny, knowing I was training hard and in a positive place when I stayed with him and trained in St. Kilda.

CHAPTER 8
FIRST LOVE

若獅子

Tiffany was my first real girlfriend. I met her through karate training when I was 16 years old and she was 15. She was an absolute stunner: tall, athletic, long-legged, with honey brown hair down to her waist and these enchanting hazel eyes. She was a very interesting mix of half Norwegian and half Maori (Pacific Islander), but 100% drop dead gorgeous.

The first time I met her was at a camp held by Shihan Eddie in countryside Victoria at Camp Buxton. These camps were held twice a year – once in summer and once in winter – a practice he inherited from the Japanese. During the camp, one time when we were eating lunch she just approached me and started talking. I was a very shy kid in those days, but she was bubbly and full of life, so I was surprised that she would even talk to me. I was thinking, "Why is this beautiful girl showing me so much attention?!" During the camp, she was around me a lot. She would approach me after training, sit down next me and start conversations. She was intelligent and always made interesting conversation, and I found her absolutely intriguing. Even though she was a lower rank than me in karate, she was a great technician. She had effortless flashy head kicks and a very positive attitude. She was never scared to mix it up with the guys during sparring, and in my eyes she was absolutely a hard-hitting, high-kicking angel.

At the start I remember looking at this beautiful girl like she was a rock star, and it wasn't too long before our puppy love turned into a real relationship, and Tiffany became my first girlfriend. Wada Sensei was at the school from the time I was about 15 to about the time I was 16-and-a-half, and Tiffany joined up about six months before Wada returned to Japan. I guess our relationship really blossomed after my superhero Wada returned to Japan. My concentration when he was there was as a karate soldier and, as I said, all of us kids would spend every possible moment of every day in his company – or as long he would put up with us, anyway. But after he left I had no real reason to be in the dojo outside of class time, so I had more time for Tiffany. We would after meet up after school, go train together, and later on – when I was about 17 or 18 – with her mum's permission, I used to spend a lot of time at her place as well. She lived just around the corner from the dojo, and since I was about two hours away, she really took over Manny's role as my sidekick and part-time caretaker.

We really were the perfect Karate Kid couple. Tiffany was my first, and I was hers, and we were both head over heels. More than just teenage love, we had this additional bond in karate, which we were both extremely passionate about. We also did a lot of normal teenage stuff, like watching TV, listening to music, walking through parks, and she was fascinated about the meaning of life. This was something I didn't give too much thought to, back then, and this really intrigued me about her. Tiffany was a natural talent and very artistic; always singing, painting, and writing poems. She loved to act and did these amazing impersonations of people. She was the perfect yin to my introvert yang. Back then, it felt like we would spend the rest of our lives together.

CHAPTER 9
THE GOD HAND

若獅子

"What I hear, I forget. What I see, I remember. What I do, I understand." –Confucius

Sosai, in Japanese, directly translates as *president* or *director general,* and appropriately, Sosai Masutatsu Oyama was many things to many people: the founder of Kyokushin Karate, pioneer of the 100-man *kumite,* inventor of the modern day full-contact tournament system, and teacher and idol to millions. To his friends and the public in general, his abbreviated name was Mas Oyama. He was Korean, and adopted the Japanese name *Oyama,* which literally translates to *big mountain.*

Sosai Oyama's worldwide fame as a karate leader was unprecedented at the time. He was a master at getting the press to sit up and take notice of his full contact, no holds barred karate style. He wrestled bulls, smashed bricks with his bare hands, knocked the tops off beer bottles with palm strikes, and had many books, films, and even a comic book series written about him. The Japanese press even named him "God Hand" in acknowledgment of his incredible strength and power.

My first hero in karate was Wada Sensei, and Wada Sensei learned all he knew from Sosai Oyama. So for me to be like him, I knew I needed to train under Sosai as well. By 16, I was already learning more and more about my Japanese master, who'd invented the style of karate I would pursue my whole life. As I've said, I had his poster above my bed, and at the front of our dojo each and every day I swore allegiance to him and the lifestyle he had developed for us. My chief source of information about Sosai was the head of my dojo and chief instructor, Shihan Eddie Emin, through his talks in the dojo, films in the summer and winter camps, and the rare book or magazine article that could be found written in English.

I relished reading every word I could find about Sosai Oyama. Many people say that Sosai was the originator of modern mixed martial arts. I know this is a bold claim, and many people lay claim to the same title, but we're talking about the 1950s here – before the phrase "mixed martial arts" even existed.

Sosai Oyama arrived in Japan in 1938, and almost immediately started training in a variety of martial arts. He trained in martial arts as varied as judo, boxing, Okinawan karate, traditional Japanese karate called Shotokan, and Goju karate, and he progressed in his training at a rate that amazed everyone. Later on, he took the best elements of each of these fighting styles to create his own style, and hence was literally mixing martial arts – which was unheard of at the time.

In 1946 Sosai Oyama read the novel *Musashi* by Ejji Yoshikawa, which is based on the exploits of Japan's most famous samurai, and both the author and the book inspired him to follow the samurai bushido code and head up into the mountains for three years of rigorous training. Among the things he took with him was a copy of Yoshikawa's book. A student named Yashiro also came with him.

The absolute solitude proved to be too much, and after six months Yashiro secretly fled during the night. It thus became even harder for Oyama, who wanted more than ever to return to civilization. So Nei Chu, founder of Goju karate, wrote to him that he should shave off an eyebrow in order to get rid of the urge. Surely he wouldn't want anyone to see him that way! He broke through the solitude by training even harder, pushing himself beyond his human limits, resolved to become the most powerful *karateka* in Japan. At night and in times of rest, Oyama would paint, write, and play the flute.

In 1947, Sosai Oyama won the karate section of the first Japanese National Martial Arts Championships. In 1950, Sosai started testing (and demonstrating) his power by fighting bulls. In all, he wrestled 52 bulls, some of which were caught on camera with old home movies. In one such film, Sosai is stabbed in the abdomen by one of the bull's' horns right away, but he keeps fighting undeterred until he wrestles the bull to the ground by its horns. It wasn't just a fun demonstration – there was a good chance the bulls would seriously injure or kill him every time – and Sosai often recalled with amusement that his first attempt to knock out a bull resulted in simply making the beast very mad. Today, of course, the animal rights groups would have something to say about these matches between man and beast, despite the fact that the animals were already destined for slaughter, and the fact that Sosai Oyama was undertaking a grave risk since he was fighting bare handed.

In 1952, Sosai travelled to the United States to display the art of karate, demonstrating for an entire year all over the country, as well as on national television. In the years to follow, he fought against professional boxers, wrestlers, and anyone else who would accept the challenge. In all, it is said Sosai fought 270 challengers, defeating every one. Of these, the vast majority were defeated with one punch! Never did a fight last more than three minutes; rarely did it take more than a few seconds to crush his opponent. His fighting principle was simple: if he got through to you, that was it.

If he hit you, you broke. If you blocked a body punch, your arm would break or dislocate. If you didn't block it, your rib was broken. Due to his superhuman power, he became known as the God Hand, a living manifestation of the Japanese warrior's maxim *"Ichi geki, hissatsu,"* or "One strike, certain death." To him, this was the true aim of technique in karate. The fancy footwork and intricate techniques were secondary (though he was also known for the power of his head kicks).

In 1956, the Oyama Karate School was first opened as the Oyama Dojo in a former ballet studio in central Tokyo. Within a short space of time membership grew to 300, and then 700 within a year. Practitioners of other styles came to train here too, eager to undertake the *jis-sen kumite* (full-contact fighting) and adopt any techniques that "would be good in a real fight." This was how Sosai Oyama's karate evolved. He took techniques from all martial arts, and did not restrict himself to karate alone. Like modern mixed martial arts, this was truly a meeting and amalgamation of fighters from different martial arts.

The Oyama Dojo members took their *kumite* seriously, seeing it primarily as a fighting art, so they expected to hit and to be hit. With few restrictions, attacking the head was common, usually with the palm heel or towel-wrapped knuckles. Grabs, throws, and groin attacks were also common. *Kumite* rounds were not timed, but would continue until one person loudly conceded defeat. Injuries occurred on a daily basis, and the dropout rate was over 90%. They had no official *do-gi*, so they just wore whatever they had. Traditional martial artists frowned upon Sosai Oyama's methods of training, so he became an outcast and pariah in the Japanese martial arts world. They even referred to his style as *jyaddo karate*, meaning "bad way" karate.

A young martial artist named Bobby Lowe saw Oyama give a demonstration in Hawaii and was stunned by his power. Soon after, he came to Japan and trained daily with him for one and a half years, becoming his first ever *uchi deshi* – meaning "live-in student." Eventually, an *uchi deshi's* time became "1,000 days for the beginning." These later *uchi deshi* became known as *Wakajishi*, or the Young Lions of Sosai Oyama, and only a few of the thousands of applicants were chosen each year for the privilege of training full-time under the Master.

It was during the 1950s that Sosai Oyama devised the 100-man *kumite*. To test his own capabilities and skills, Sosai decided to do a 300-man *kumite*: 100 fights each day, over three successive days. He chose the strongest students in his dojo, who were to fight him one at a time until they'd all had a turn, and then they'd start from the beginning again, until the three hundred rounds were up. He defeated them all, never wavering

The God Hand

in his resolve, despite the fact that he himself suffered severe physical injury in the process.

Having set the example, Sosai Oyama started to institute the 100-man *kumite* as a requirement for attaining 4th or 5th *dan*. He soon found, however, that not everyone had the spirit to do it, though the physical skill could easily be taught. The indomitable will, courage, and determination – the "Spirit of *Osu*" in its extreme – just wasn't to be found in everyone. Thus it became an invitation-only event, a true honor for those few who had the right stuff. Only a small number of people have ever completed the 100-man *kumite* since Sosai Oyama (19 at the time of this writing), a testament to just how incredibly difficult a challenge it is.

On May 22, 1965, Steve Arneil, a world-class fighter and Kyokushin legend from England, became the first person to complete the 100-man *kumite* after Oyama himself. The 100-man *kumite* took him around two hours and 45 minutes to complete, with each round scheduled to take one minute and 30 seconds (but a round ended if he managed to knock down his opponent). In an interview in 2005, Arneil said, "I did not have to beat everyone I fought; that would have been ridiculous! I just had to keep going, I had to have the spirit not to give up, no matter what they threw at me."

The popularity of Sosai Oyama's karate grew almost as fast as the legend of the man himself and the accomplishments of his students. The current world headquarters building, or *Honbu*, officially opened in June 1964. It was at this time that Oyama Karate adopted the name *Kyokushin*, meaning "Ultimate Truth." In the same year, the International Karate Organization (IKO) was inaugurated. After formally establishing the *Kyokushin Kaikan* in 1964, Sosai Oyama directed the organization through a period of expansion.

Oyama handpicked instructors who displayed ability in promoting the style and gaining new members. He would choose an instructor to open a new dojo, and the instructor would move to that town and demonstrate his karate skills in public places. After that, word of mouth would spread through the local area until the dojo had a dedicated core of students.

Oyama also sent instructors to other countries such as the Netherlands, Australia, the United States of America, the United Kingdom, and Brazil to spread Kyokushin in the same way. Many students also travelled to Japan to train with Oyama. It is estimated that over the last 50 years, Kyokushin Karate practitioners have numbered more than 12 million in 140 countries, becoming one of the largest martial arts organizations in the world.

Sosai Mas Oyama was really a legend in his own lifetime. He was a true visionary, a great teacher, a charismatic leader, and a master of publicity and the media. Sosai's achievements became folklore, and his status as leader of the largest karate organization in the world meant he was revered and worshipped by millions. This was the beginning of the 30-year golden age of Kyokushin Karate.

By the time I was training karate in 1984, Kyokushin had officially been around for 20 years. I was lucky enough to be a part of the last 10 years of that golden age, and felt very privileged to be involved in a sport that was still in its infancy in Australia. I was convinced that one day I would meet and train under the great master Sosai Mas Oyama. I would go to Japan and become one of his *uchi deshi,* or Young Lion.

CHAPTER 10
MY QUEST TO BECOME AN UCHI DESHI

若獅子

"*Uchi deshi*" means "live-in student," and in my time in Kyokushin Karate it was a 1,000-day program of training all day, every day. Sosai Oyama designed the 1,000-day *uchi deshi* program to replicate the three years of solitary training he himself undertook in the mountains on Chiba in the late 1940s, to perfect the art that years later became Kyokushin Karate. The few students chosen to enter the program were known as the "*wakajishi*," or Young Lions. Thousands of young kids applied each year to become one of Sosai Oyama's Young Lions, but each year less than 10 inductees were accepted. It was my dream to enter that program, and no matter what, I was going to make that dream come true.

By this stage we were training in the new dojo in Elwood out behind the squash courts under Shihan Eddie, but my personal idol was Wada. Shihan Eddie was the school owner and was a hands-on teacher, but in those days he had a serious knee injury, so having Wada teaching in-house and demonstrating these incredible techniques was just an amazingly lucky turn of fate for me. And I was always contemplating that if Wada was a student of Sosai Oyama, and Wada was this good, then imagine how good Sosai Oyama was? Six months into Wada's term, I had convinced myself that I was going to be an *uchi deshi* just like him. On those long train rides home, I would write in my diary, "I WILL BE AN *UCHI DESHI* OF SOSAI OYAMA," every day.

The first thing I did to set myself on this path was to tell my mum and Peter that my dream was to go to Japan and live there for three years as an *uchi deshi* under Sosai Oyama. By now, mum knew who Wada Sensei and Sosai Oyama were because I constantly talked about them both, probably driving her batty with my obsession. I was about 17 at this stage, and halfway through my second attempt at Year 11. She knew I was a karate fanatic and at the start, like any mum, she was probably a little concerned, but I remember her as always being very encouraging and supportive. So when I told them my dream, both my mum and Rizza said, "OK, Judd, run with it. If you can get there, get there."

Next, I approached Wada Sensei. This was a couple of months before he was going to return to Japan. I said to him in simple English, "I want to be an *uchi deshi* like you. I want to go to Japan and study karate for three years under Sosai," and his reaction was very supportive. He said, "Sure, Judd, sure." in his broken English.

Remember that Wada and I had a great relationship, and he really liked me. He also believed in my abilities and discipline, as a year earlier he had told me, "One day you are going to be Australian champion."

Wada told me to write a letter that he would take back with him to Japan, to give to Sosai Oyama with Shihan Eddie's blessing, and a letter from him as well. Wada also promised me he would give Sosai his recommendation. I was a completely overwhelmed by this, and my hopes were very high. My dream and plan to get to Japan were taking shape.

About a month after Wada returned to Japan, I got a letter from *Honbu* dojo delivered to my family home in Strathmore saying, basically, "Yes, we have received letters from Wada and Shihan, and yes, you have been accepted into the *uchi deshi* program." His secretary probably typed this up, as it was in English, but was clearly signed with Sosai Mas Oyama's signature. I was absolutely ecstatic and completely over the moon.

Not long after this, Shihan Eddie called my mum and me into the dojo to sign the official Japanese paperwork. It was very lengthy and all in Japanese, and I have no idea what it actually said, but I knew it was part of the formality of joining as an *uchi deshi* and I filled out all the forms as marked, and signed everywhere that was required.

Shihan Eddie was very proud of me, and he said as much, but he also told me how hard this was going to be, and that I should be prepared for great hardships. I was going to be representing his dojo, and the Japanese way is that if you recommend someone, then the responsibility lies on that person's shoulders. Should something go wrong in any way, even 10 years down the track, the blame would come back to the person making the recommendation. This is simply the Japanese way.

There was only one obstacle left before I could become an *uchi deshi*. Sosai had requested that I wait a year before coming, as ideally he wanted his *uchi deshi* to be around 18 to 20, and I was still just 17. This was not the problem, though; I could wait a year. The obstacle was that I needed to raise the equivalent of $10,000 US dollars to cover basic food and board for the three-year course. It doesn't seem like much these days, but in the 1980s $10,000 (about $15,000 in Australian dollars) was a lot of money – and, more importantly, money my mum and I didn't have. However, I did get some help almost immediately from the local media.

Just after the OK came through, the local press got hold of the story. The story of my acceptance into this exclusive karate program in Japan ended up in a few of the local community newspapers, and then Melbourne's largest newspaper, and even onto the biggest current affairs show of the time, *The Hinch Program*. The news back in those days tended to concentrate more on the positive aspects of life, and this was a great story for them. All the stories talked about my dream and dedication, and the need for funding to make it happen. With hundreds or even thousands of people now knowing my story, there was no turning back!

CHAPTER 11
WELCOME TO
THE 100-MAN FIGHT

若獅子

The 100-man *kumite* originated with Sosai Masutatsu Oyama in the 1950s, as a way to test the fighting skills he developed and taught with Kyokushin Karate. The first one to undertake the 100-man *kumite*, Oyama not only successfully fought 100 black belts and martial arts practitioners in a row, he completed the feat three times over three consecutive days!

The word '*kumite*' or *hyakunin kumite* in Japanese literally translates to "'grappling hands,"' and is part of the three main facets of training in karate, along with *kata* (forms) and *kihon* (fundamentals). Back in those days, head punches, groin strikes, and just about anything else was in allowed, and it truly was a blood sport. But the *kumite* started to take on more structure by the time Kyokushin Karate disciple Steve Arneil finished it in 1965, the first person other than Sosai Oyama to do so.

Over the decades many tried, but only 19 have endured the 100-fight trial to the finish – great fighters and men like Howard Collins, Masada Akira, Francisco Filo, and Yamaki Kenji to name a few, and Naomi Ali in 2004, the first women to record the milestone.

As for me, I never thought much about the *kumite* during my career, though it would have been more prudent to attempt it in my athletic prime, and not at 40 years old. But I guess it was always in the back of my consciousness, as I remember Sosai Oyama instilled in us Young Lions that there were two accomplishments every great karate fighter should pursue in his lifetime:

1) To be a world champion, and
2) To complete the 100-man *kumite*.

After winning some and losing some in many tournaments throughout my career, I finally achieved the first of these goals in 2010, winning the World Championship of Karate belt as a heavyweight – a long way from the skinny kid that entered Sosai's *uchi deshi* program. So what was next for me?

That's when someone brought up the idea to do the second on Oyama's list of life accomplishments: the *kumite*.

When I was first asked to do the 100-man fight, my first reaction was, "No way. I can't do it." I thought it was way too hard. To fight 100 consecutive opponents – other black belts and professional fighters, no less – with no headgear, no gloves, and no one pulling their punches or kicks, was insane. Each fight would go on for one and a half minutes, or until I knocked out or knocked down my opponent, and I couldn't stop the fights or take a break for any reason without instantly being disqualified. A doctor would be onsite, but not allowed to help me for any reason until the fight was over. I'd only have a short time between fights – only 10 to 15 seconds, or enough for my next opponent to come out, both of us to bow to the referee and each other, and for a couple of short periods throughout for my corner to check on me and give me advice.

I was damn hesitant to say 'yes', as I'd seen what the *kumite* did to some of the best fighters in the world, including someone I respected: Masada Akira."

In fact, I'd participated in the *kumite* as a fighter when Akira attempted it years earlier, and I had fought him twice – in round 10, when he was fresh, and then again in round 70. By then Akira was delirious, a walking punching bag whose mind and body were in shock. It was more like fighting a wounded animal, and he even started biting opponents, going into primal survival mode.

So I kept turning down suggestions that I do the 100-man fight, but at the same time, the idea had taken root and started to grow, as I knew it was what Sosai wanted of his fighters – the last ultimate challenge to define us.

So when I was officially invited to compete in the 100-man *kumite* in 2011, I said yes.

My *kumite* would be held on October 22, 2011 – about 7 months away – in a dojo beneath Osaka's Prefectural Gymnasium in Japan.

What the hell had I gotten myself into?

CHAPTER 12
JUDD REID, THE CHALKIE

若獅子

I was officially accepted into the *uchi deshi* program a couple of months after Wada returned to Japan in 1988. Some news articles and a TV segment covered my story, explaining that I needed the funds from the public or a sponsor to get to Japan and to cover the costs of the three-year program. In order to enter the *uchi deshi* course, I needed to come up with about $10,000 USD to pay for my tuition. Looking back, it was a just a nominal fee and would have barely covered feeding me, but in 1988 as a 17-year-old kid, it was money I didn't have. Also, I had heard that 17 was considered too young to join the program, from the Japanese perspective, as they preferred me to be at least 18 or 19 when I arrived, so I had a little extra time to raise the funds. Finding a way to raise money for the Young Lions course became my mission.

I spoke to my mum about this, and she had a friend with connections at the Melbourne Stock Exchange who said that they were looking for a "chalkie" on the trading floor. In those days the stock market still had a physical trading floor – unlike today where everything is done by computer. I had just finished Year 11 at school, and with my mum's permission I quit school and immediately started to work.

I loved my job as a chalkie from the beginning. To this day it was still my favorite job, outside of karate. Let me explain what a chalkie does. I would start at about 8:30 each morning, since the trading hours were from 10 AM to 4 PM. My job was to write down the bids and offers on the trading board that were being yelled at me by the traders from all the big banks and brokerages, who were standing on the trading floor taking orders. As part of this job I had to be able to recognize not just the bids and offers above all the other shouting, but I also the voices of the people they came from. I would then write up those bids and offers as quickly as possible on the chalkboard, with annotation next to the number representing the name of the person or organization who had yelled the bid. I was basically the human market maker. And to do this very important job that made and lost people millions of dollars, I carried my high tech tools of the trade: a duster in my left hand, and a piece of chalk in my right.

The trading board was about six feet high and about 100 feet long, up in an elevated position that could be seen by all in the exchange, with the trading floor (or pit) below us. The left side of the board was for mining stocks, the right side industrials, and in the middle financials. The busiest and most traded stocks were right in the middle, and I guess I was pretty good at what I did because I was assigned to the middle only about three months after I started. As the bid and offers were matched, I scrubbed them off the board, and as new bids and offers were made, I wrote them up. In those days the market used to stop for an hour for lunch, and this was our only break. It was hard work, lots of pressure and chaotic, but very exciting and I loved it.

The brokers were unforgiving characters, I remember, and if we messed up we really copped it. Of course, our mistakes meant they would lose money so I can understand why, but this wasn't a job for the thin-skinned or someone who couldn't withstand pressure. Most of the brokers were pretty good guys, but I remember one particular broker who, if one of the chalkies made a mistake, would yell out at the top of his lungs "Punk, Punk, Punk, Punk…" until absolutely everyone knew which chalkie had messed up, and was shamed and made to look foolish.

The hardest part of the trading day was the last five minutes when everyone wanted to get their final bids in. I remember all us chalkies had a great relationship together – we were all teenagers about the same age, and a few minutes before that final burst of insane action we would huddle and put our fists together, yelling the words, "Wonder Twins, powers activate form of Super Chalkie!" and then run back to our positions to close out the day.

They were great times. It was a great job, a great rush, and I guarantee that almost all the other chalkies went on to successful careers as stockbrokers. I wonder what they thought of me having this very sought-after job, yet using it as a stepping-stone to a life in karate, something completely different than their own dreams. But although I loved the job and the excitement, karate was always my calling, and I look back with no regrets whatsoever.

I never actually got any funding for the *uchi deshi* course from outside sources, nor any rich benefactor. But over the course of that year, between the job my mum got me and the dojo organizing a number of fundraisers, I finally got most of the funds together at the end of 1989. In the end, I never got 100% of the money. I got to about $8,000.

CHAPTER 13
BLACK BELT GRADING

若獅子

At the end of 1989, I did my black belt grading. Even though I was working full time at the stock exchange, I was also training five days a week in karate. In order to build myself up for the challenges ahead, I also began training at a local weightlifting gym with my old schoolmate, Nick Murphy, and his mate and training partner, Anton Cavka.

Anton was only a couple of years older than me, but he was built like a monster in those days: 210 pounds (95 kg) of pure muscle. He and Nick both trained like men possessed. Their idol was Arnold Schwarzenegger, and Anton used to say he wanted to be like Franco Colombo – so strong that if a car got in his way, rather than walk around it, he would pick it up and move it out of the way. Anton was a funny guy with a very unique outlook on life, full of confidence, and zero fear of trying anything and everything. We got along famously.

I was a skinny kid in those days, and the idea was to put on some strength and size so that the Japanese fighters in the dojo wouldn't be able to push me around. However, someone forgot to tell me that training five times a week in karate and three times on the weights, without eating huge amounts of food, would make it difficult to put on any real size. I think I only gained a few pounds, and went from 145 pounds (66 kg) to close to 155 (70 kg) that year, but I certainly got a lot stronger. Anton and Nick concentrated on very high intensity training and did lots of super sets, always to failure, trying to beat their personal best in every session. The gym was a rough old place, full of some of Melbourne's toughest security guards and bouncers, and we were just kids compared to them. They gave us a lot of stick, but we gave it right back, so it was all in good fun and the place had a great atmosphere.

Other than weightlifting, Manny and I teamed up and trained like crazy men at karate during the last six months of 1989, in the lead-up to our black belt grading. We were both brown belts and determined to succeed on our most important day. We did lots of cardio – hill sprints, swimming, and interval training on the bike outside of karate class – and were as prepared as we could be when the grading day finally came.

In fact, we were so fit that we conquered each and every challenge thrown at us by Shihan Eddie in his eight hours of torture to get our prized *shodan* (black belt first *dan*).

I received my black belt in November 1989, in the Elwood dojo in front of all my classmates, awarded by Shihan Eddie Emin after almost seven years of training. It was the greatest honor of my life, up 'til that point, and the timing seemed like destiny, as I was due to leave for Japan in the New Year. I would be saying goodbye to some great old friends in the dojo including Manny, Tommy, Zav, Trifon, Nick, Emin, and Anton Vojic (not my mate, weightlifting Anton), and poor Tiffany, who was still my girlfriend, but who I was abandoning to chase my dream in Japan. Shihan Eddie was – and still is – a true pioneer of Kyokushin Karate in Australia, and still runs his own school in Moorabbin, Melbourne. He is 88 now, and still going strong. Without him I would never have discovered Kyokushin Karate, and it seemed fitting that he oversaw my training all the way to getting my black belt – just before my life changed forever, yet again.

CHAPTER 14
SACRIFICING EVERYTHING FOR MY DREAM

若獅子

It was early May 1990, and after some delays in getting my visa, I was finally leaving for Japan. My whole extended family came to the airport to give me a sendoff, including my family, karate schoolmates, and friends – about 20 people in total. I was so happy I could finally get on the plane, and wanted to arrive in Japan as quickly as possible. I'd been overseas to the UK, France, Holland, Ireland, and New Zealand, but I'd never been to Asia, and this was going to be different. This wasn't going to be a holiday, but my sole goal in life – all I'd been dreaming about for the past four years.

At the time, it didn't dawn on me how monumental a life-changing experience this was going to be. I was leaving a great neighborhood and lifestyle in my home country and entering a completely foreign culture and language where I would be a total stranger and outsider. My life in Australia had a great deal of promise and opportunity, but I was risking everything by giving it all up and starting over from nothing.

I was walking away from life as a chalkie, which really could have been a stepping-stone to a career as stockbroker and potentially millions of dollars. But at the Melbourne Stock Exchange, I didn't think about this at all. All I could think about was my dream of going to Japan and being a full time *karateka*. I wonder what the brokers thought of all this? They must have thought I was crazy.

I had an incredibly supportive mother who meant everything to me. With Rizza and Marnie, I had a very strong family base – not to mention all of my karate friends, and my best mate, Murph. And I was leaving all this behind to chase a dream in a country I knew little about, where I wouldn't have even one person I truly knew.

But at the time, I didn't even think about any of that. I was just a young kid with an incredible dream, and that was all that mattered. As a kid you never really consider the "what ifs" or consequences, and it wasn't until many years later that I was able to reflect on the impact this decision had on my life.

But without a doubt, the hardest thing I had to do emotionally was leave the love of my life, Tiffany. Walking away from beautiful Tiffany was difficult for me, but I have to admit it was crushing for her. I was so fanatical about karate that everything else came a distant second – including my first love. While Tiffany knew I wanted to go to Japan from the first day she met me, and she really encouraged me, deep down I know she wished I would change my mind and stay behind with her. So once I had the funds saved to be able to set a date to leave for Japan in 1990, Tiffany and I began to drift apart. In the weeks before I left, I remember a lot of crying and tears, and I felt really bad. We swore our love to each other, and said that three years was not that long a time, so we would be together again once I got back. But Tiffany was a deep thinker and more of a realist than me, and in the last few weeks she put up a bit of a wall, so we saw less of each other. I look back now and understand that that was her way of protecting herself. The last time I saw Tiffany was about a week before I left for Japan, and I still remember her as this supermodel karate fighter and a very beautiful person.

I remember it was early evening after a nice, sunny day when I got to Melbourne Airport, with two old suitcases filled to the brim with my karate *gi'*, running shoes, summer clothes and some heavy winter clothes, a handful of photographs of my family and friends, and a few special gifts and ornaments some people had given me for good luck. So after many lengthy goodbyes and tears from my mum and aunty at the gate, I finally I got on the "Flying Kangaroo" plane that roared down the runway and lifted into the sunset before banking north toward Tokyo.

CHAPTER 15
ENTER THE DRAGON

若獅子

  The flight to Japan took about 10 hours, though I checked my watch every twenty minutes and calculated how long until we landed. I was so excited that I couldn't sleep the whole way there. I looked out the window as we floated through the clouds over the Sea of Japan, picturing all of the faces of my friends and family I was leaving behind. When we finally touched down and I stepped off the plane at Narita Airport, it was a surreal experience. It felt like I'd landed on a different planet. All the signs were written in Japanese and no one spoke English, so I just followed the crowd and did what they did. I had a cultural visa stamp in my passport that I'd applied for from Australia, and immigration looked at it, stamped it, and sent me on my way.

  I got on the train from the airport, which is about one and a half hours from central Tokyo, and made my own way to the west exit of Ikebukuro Station. Everything looked so well organized and clean; it looked like I was on a different planet. I had the *Honbu* (the name of the Kyokushin headquarters) address written down in Japanese, thanks to one of the Japanese students at Shihan Eddie's dojo. I stepped into a taxi outside the train station, and the taxi took me straight to the place that would be my new home – which ended up being only about five minutes away. Out of the taxi window, I watched the streets bustle with the Japanese eager to start their day and get to work, as it was 7:30 in the morning.

  I got out of the taxi with my luggage in front of a five-story building with *Kyokushin Kaikan* in Japanese writing on a huge banner on the side of the building. Although this was the first time I saw the headquarters of the Kyokushin *Kaikan* in real life, Manny had shown me pictures from a trip he made there in 1987 from the world tournaments. Suddenly, it really hit me that I was finally here. I'd been looking at pictures of this building in books and magazines for four years, and now I was standing in front of it in absolute awe. My heart raced and my hands were sweaty, and I made sure my t-shirt was neatly tucked in before I took a step forward.

A narrow road led to the entrance of the building. As I started walking down it, a young Japanese kid with a shaved head dressed in a Kyokushin tracksuit literally ran at me and said something in Japanese, which I obviously didn't understand. I later learned he was a first-year *uchi deshi* by the name of Suzuki. He immediately grabbed my luggage from me and walked at a brisk pace to the entrance of the *Honbu,* and at the entrance I encountered another Japanese guy – Kato, standing on guard in *fudo dachi* (meaning standing at attention with his feet together, elbows tucked in, and forearms and fists pointing straight ahead). Only later did I realize that there were always two *uchi deshi* guards at the entrance in case rival karate organizations attacked, which I never saw but was common in the old days.

Suzuki and Kato spoke to each other in Japanese, which again I didn't understand. Suzuki gestured to me as if to say, "follow me," and then proceeded to run down the street. I ran as well to keep up. He still had my luggage and was literally sprinting away with it, and I had no idea where we were going. We ran around the whole building and block, about 120 yards, to reach the dormitory at the back. Suzuki reached the dormitory first and opened the traditional Japanese sliding door, immediately yelling *osu shitsureishimasu,* which means, "please excuse me," in the most polite form. He took off his shoes and left them neatly outside, and I did the same. He bowed and yelled *osu* again so I mimicked him, knowing only that word from the dojo and otherwise having no idea what he was saying.

This was the ground floor where there was a dining room with a big long table, and the kitchen separated by a curtain. Inside the kitchen there was a fridge, a massive rice cooker, and a small area for cooking. The kitchen, like the rest of the dormitory, was very old but immaculately clean. Standing inside this small kitchen was an older lady, about 65, who I later found out was Robo San, the cook. She was our home-away-from-home mum. She cooked the food every day except Sunday. Suzuki and I walked through to the end of the dining room, where there were two doors – one leading to a staircase, and the other leading to a bedroom for the third-year or senior *uchi deshi*.

Suzuki opened the door to go upstairs and went through the same routine, bowing and yelling *osu* and *shitsureishimasu* again. The stairway was incredibly steep and narrow, unlike anything you'd ever see in the west. It was about 20 steps to the top, and Suzuki was carrying two of my bags – which, in hindsight, were incredibly heavy. To this day, it's hard to imagine how a guy of Suzuki's slender frame got them up that staircase.

My mind was racing, as I still had no idea what was going on. I didn't speak any Japanese, they didn't speak any English, and all I had to go by were some gestures Suzuki made at the front entrance, so I just tried to follow his instructions in a language I couldn't understand.

At the top of the staircase there were more rooms: three bedrooms, and two toilets behind closed doors.

Suzuki opened the door to one of the rooms and once again yelled *osu* and that same phrase in Japanese. I again mimicked him by yelling *osu,* and we entered the room. With a quick survey of the room I saw there were traditional Japanese tatami mats on the floor and sliding cupboards where everything, including futons and bedding, were stored. Tatami mats are made out of straw or bamboo, and have a particular smell; the closest comparison I can think of is the smell of hay, and this hit me straight away. This was the main bedroom for the first year *uchi deshi* and it was basically one big room with a wooden pillar in the middle, and sliding frosted windows down the right-hand side. I remember seeing a small set of shelves on the left-hand side filled with Kyokushin "Power Karate" magazines in Japanese.

There were two or three other Japanese guys, and three foreigners in the room. Suzuki said something to one of the foreigners, and then yelled *osu* and left the room. The one he spoke to came over and introduced himself as Mohamad. In broken English, he said he was from France and that the Japanese called him Mokodomo, as they couldn't pronounce his real name. Next, an American guy came over and introduced himself as Nathan Ligo, and a third said he was Sandor Brezovai from Hungary. The Japanese, on the other hand, just continued to sit and talk amongst themselves.

I said *osu* to everyone and shook each of their hands, including the Japanese who spoke no English. They seemed busy, so I left them to their own devices. Ligo, however, started talking to me, asking typical questions about where I was from and whether I was feeling tired from the trip, and then he went on to explain to me the rules and workings of the dormitory. He was a friendly guy, but basically we skipped the chitchat and went straight into the business of the *uchi deshi* and the dormitory. Ligo produced a piece of paper, nominating himself as the person to introduce me to the rules of dormitory life. He went over the rules, etiquette, and behavior expected of a live-in student. For example, when entering or exiting the dormitory you must always yell *osu* and say *shitsureishimasu* (the most formal and polite way of saying "'excuse me'" in Japanese). The same goes for if you see one your *Senpais* (senior students).

I already knew a lot of the dojo and Kyokushin etiquette from my time under Shihan Eddie, but the dormitory etiquette was another level. The rules and hierarchy were more involved than I could possibly imagine. I had to try to remember the hierarchy of the sleeping quarters, laying out our shoes at the front door, etc. Ligo handed me the piece of paper with all of the basic rules written on it in English and said, "Learn this very quickly, because we've got breakfast in 30 minutes." There were many rules for interacting with the other *uchi deshi*. Upon sighting any senior student, we immediately had to bow, yell *osu*, and if we walked past them we also had to yell *shitsureishimasu*. A good example of the military nature of the rules I remember was the very last one. It stated that if you were sitting on the tatami and a senior entered the room, you would immediately have to jump up, yell *osu*, and stand at attention until the senior acknowledged and told you to stand at ease or relax. If he chose not to tell you to stand at ease, you could be standing there for an awfully long time.

I put my luggage away in one of the cupboards, sat down on the tatami mats, and tried to process what Ligo had written out for me. Everything was so new and overwhelming, it was dizzying. Even something as simple as going to the bathroom was an adventure. When I walked into the bathroom my first day in the dorm, I looked down to discover there wasn't a toilet like I was used to, but just a hole in the ground, as is the Japanese custom. I didn't even know which way to face, or how to position myself! There was so much information to take in that I had no chance of even getting through half of what was written before breakfast, but I took in as much as I could. I wanted to prove that I was going to give it my best shot and become one of them.

Soon enough Ligo said, "Let's go to breakfast," so I followed him downstairs to the dining room. In the dining room was a long table with enough chairs for at least 20 people. When we entered at exactly 8 AM there were about 12 people already standing in front of their chairs. Ligo guided me to a seat where, not wanting to be out of place, I waited to see what everyone else was going to do. Everyone stood in front of their seats, facing the front, and from out of nowhere one of the Japanese started yelling out a series of phrases that the rest of the group repeated loudly. These were the rules and regulations of the dormitory in Japanese. I stood mute at attention and tried to listen to what was being said.

THE YOUNG LIONS

One of the Japanese head *Senpai* pressed play on this huge black ghetto blaster in the middle of the table, and everyone burst into very loud singing – again in Japanese. I didn't know it then, but they were singing The Young Lions ballad, which would be sung before every breakfast for the next three years of my time as an *uchi deshi*. As we repeated the oath and looked to the front of the dining room we saw three things: a number of framed pictures of Sosai Oyama along the walls, the dormitory rules dead center at the front, and the words to the *Wakajishi Ryo Ryoka* (The Young Lions dormitory song) on the right. Breakfast began at 8 AM each day, and with the dining room being filled with 10 to 20 screaming *uchi deshi*, this must have been one hell of an alarm clock for the surrounding densely packed neighborhood.

A bunch of first-years brought all the food out of the kitchen and laid it on the table. In front of each person there was a big bowl of rice, a miso soup, something wrapped in this green paper-like substance, an egg, and some foul smelling food I couldn't recognize. Everything seemed so organized.

Someone yelled out yet another phrase I didn't understand, but in this case Ligo had written it down and told me that it was compulsory to say this before each meal. The phrase was *itadakimasu*, which doesn't really have a translation in English, but might be best described as "let's begin eating."

Eating was done with military precision. It seemed there was an order to everything, and I was the only one who didn't know it. Everyone cracked open the raw egg over the rice, stirred it in a bit with the chopsticks, poured the miso soup in, poured the *natto* (foul smelling stuff) in, and then placed the *nori* (stuff wrapped in green paper) on top. Then they all picked up their bowls, held them to their mouths, and shoveled food in with the chopsticks in record time. Everyone finished breakfast in less than two minutes. There was no chitchat, no looking around. I gave a little laugh inside, as I finally understood where Wada Sensei had learned his eating habits.

When we finished eating, everyone yelled another phrase

that Ligo had written down. This one was *gochisosamadeshita,* another phrase with no real English equivalent, but perhaps the closest would be "thank you for the feast." I've got to say I felt stupid and clumsy trying to repeat these phrases, even though they were written down in front of me. Everything was confusing, and I felt completely lost.

Just about everyone got up and disappeared after finishing breakfast, and Ligo tapped my shoulder and motioned for me to follow him. We went back upstairs to our living quarters, and Ligo told me to get ready for *chori,* meaning morning ceremony, with Sosai at 9:30 AM. I was jumping with excitement to be only minutes away from meeting the man to whom I had sworn allegiance for all these years. My head was still spinning from the long flight, lack of sleep, and all that had happened in the first two hours since I'd been in Japan, but I surveyed the area that was to be my home for the next three years.

The dining room on the first floor was like none other I'd seen, about 10 meters long but very narrow, only 2 meters wide, and could fit about 20 people. Also on the first floor was the third-year senior students' room, about six tatami mats in size that could sleep a maximum of four people.

On the second floor, up the very steep staircase, sat three rooms – one for the first-years, which was about 12 tatami mats in size and could sleep about 12; one for second-year students that was about eight tatami mats large and could sleep six to eight; and next to that room was a single two-tatami mat room where one person could comfortably sleep. But this room was empty, as the widely held superstition was that the room was cursed. It was whispered that everyone who stayed in this room had some form of bad luck befall them, so all of the *uchi deshi* refused to stay in there. It remained empty except for when we occasionally had short-term visitors – who we 'never told about our somewhat odd superstition. I remember that there was a lot of handwritten graffiti on the walls of that empty room, as well. It was the only room where you could find graffiti, which was very unusual for Japan, and especially within the immaculate dormitory it seemed out of place. Most of the graffiti was in Japanese, and still to this day I don't know exactly what it all said, but I like to think they were warnings and incantations to scare away Japanese evil spirits. I also remember there was a large bit of graffiti written on the wall in English that said, "When the going gets tough, the tough get going."

Thankfully, I was told that I would be sleeping on a futon next to Ligo, and given space in the cupboard for my personal belongings. Then I was told to get ready for the morning cermony with Sosai Oyama.

CHAPTER 16
MEETING MY MASTER

若獅子

People often ask me about the first time I met Sosai Mas Oyama, and what my first impressions of him were, but I find it difficult to put into a few words. After all, he's looked upon as a superhuman Japanese karate god in many circles. Like I mentioned, his nickname in the press was "God Hand," and Sosai Oyama had comic books, movies, and even a regular animated TV show made about him. The man was a living legend, and sometimes that makes it hard to separate fact from fiction. But with Sosai, I can truly say it was an honor to get to know the real man behind the mythical persona, and I'll only share what I experienced personally.

I met Sosai Mas Oyama for the first time two hours after I arrived in Japan, on May 1990, just after breakfast. The *uchi deshi* would have a meeting with Sosai every morning at 9:30 AM in the dojo called *chore,* meaning "morning ceremony." The purpose of this meeting was for Sosai to give a talk to the *uchi deshi*, offering guidance, encouragement to train harder, and setting us on the right path for the day.

At my first meeting, I stood there in my tracksuit pants and t-shirt with my long hair, extremely nervous about meeting the person I'd idolized for years. All the other students were also in sports sweats, as karate *gi* were reserved for classes. As soon as Sosai Oyama came into the dojo, he greeted us with *osu*. He then strode straight up and welcomed me in English – which he spoke a little bit, although his understanding was much better. I distinctly remember he said, "Welcome to Japan. Is everything OK? Welcome to the *uchi deshi* course." I answered with a loud *osu* and then he went to the front of the group and gave his daily speech to the whole group of *uchi deshi*.

Sosai stood in front of the *uchi deshi*, dressed smartly in a business suit. He always wore this classy style of suit that was popular in the 60s and 70s, along with a formal overcoat and a hat. He was also wearing his trademark large glasses. This was just his style. I was totally exhausted and overwhelmed but full of adrenaline, standing stiffly at attention, staring at my new master, and trying to take in as much as I could. Sosai was about 5'10", 200 pounds (91 kg), with a big barrel chest and very muscular, just as I had seen in all the magazines. I didn't understand what he was saying, but I remember he spoke in a very loud, confident voice, and his facial expressions gave me the impression that he was a kind-hearted person. As he spoke, he made eye contact with all of the *uchi deshi*. He had this incredible aura about him, and I was totally transfixed – as was everyone else in the room. The *chore* lasted about 10 minutes, after which Sosai said *osu* and all of us erupted in a huge *osu* in reply. Sosai then strode over to exit the dojo. He turned to us, bowed, and said *osu*, and we all yelled *osu* again and pivoted 45 degrees to face him as he departed up the stairs to his office.

I had finally met and greeted the man I'd idolized for years, and he was everything I expected and more. This description will have to suffice for now, though I promise to share more later on, as no man – especially Sosai – can be completely captured by a first impression. I'd have more than 1,000 days over three years to get to know this great man, and I will have many more chances to tell you who he was, through his own words and actions.

CHAPTER 17
HAJIME! STARTING THE 100-MAN FIGHT

若獅子

  I had trained like a man possessed for four months in Thailand, working out for six hours a day, six days a week. Day after day, I pushed my body to new limits, reaching new levels of conditioning in anticipation of the pounding I'd have to take, doing heavy weight training, carrying huge logs, sprinting up steep hills, completing burpees with a man on my back, pounding the heavy bag for an hour straight, and letting other fighters tee off on me with punches and kicks while I stood still, defenseless, and absorbed them.

  Most days I lost 10 pounds or more just from sweating in the oppressive Thai heat. There were countless nights where I would toss and turn at night, not being able to sleep properly because my body was in pain, exhausted with lactic acid buildup everywhere, especially in my legs.

  Ten days out I tapered off my training. This is a very important part of the process. On the day of the event you need to be jumping out of your skin. Michael Dugina, my old mentor, used to say to me, "Judd you have done all the hard work already. You can't get any fitter one week before your competition, but you might get more tired, even totally exhausted, and of course that's the last thing you want." So I followed his advice. I shortened my sessions, got plenty of rest, and was feeling stronger, sharper, and more and more ready to go as each day drew closer.

  I arrived in Osaka three days before the big event. I was feeling great, had zero jet lag and was totally refreshed. I had pushed myself that hard for so long that with this period of tapering off and rest I literally felt invincible. I was ready!

With my mum, sister, and good friends that came over to support me, I was totally at ease and feeling zero stress. It seemed strange that in earlier days I would have been exhausted from the flight, hazy in my thinking, and just running on pure adrenaline. This time I was the most relaxed I could ever remember. The night before the big day, I had a great sleep of about eight hours. I had a massive breakfast and a big lunch at an Italian restaurant in Osaka called Capricciosa. I remember sitting there with Ned and the guys. Ned was cracking jokes and I wasn't saying much, but I felt great. The boys really made me feel relaxed, and I ate a huge bowl of pasta.

The start of the 100-man *kumite* was at 5 PM. We arrived there about an hour or so before it began. I was still very relaxed, but my mind started slowly tuning in to the big mission I had in front of me. I thought about all the sacrifice and punishment I had put myself through. There was no cloudiness in my mind. I was finely tuned and believed in myself 100 percent, and so did my supporters. I was doing this for them, too, and for Sosai. Actually, I was doing this for them first and foremost, and only secondly for myself, and there was no way I was going to let anyone down.

The dojo slowly started to fill up and the fighters changed into their *gi* and began warming up. I warmed up as well, stretched, did some shadow fighting and light sparring, playing around with Phil. Nick came up to me and whispered in my ear to take it easy and not to get injured. It was very sound advice, but I was just getting my eye in and was feeling great.

Sugihara Kancho stood up at the head of the officials' table and gave a brief introduction as to what was about to take place. To tell you the truth, I can't remember what he said, because by this time I was in my own world. I was calm, but ready to switch on like a Formula One racecar. I wouldn't normally say this to anyone, but'' I really felt like the strongest man on the planet. No one was going to hurt me, and I was going to teach these fighters and put on a display as a teacher might to his students. I was senior to almost all of my opponents, and I was going to beat every last one of them. This is how I felt, and it was the mindset I was going to need to get through this feat.

The judge called me into the center of the mat, and we were about to commence. Phil had drawn fighter number one, so my old training partner and student was my first fight. We had a laugh about this. It's on YouTube, and Phil's face is priceless when his name is drawn out of a hat as the number one fighter.

"*Hajime!*" the judge yelled out, and the fight began. I moved forward. Phil tried some combinations to muscle me back, but I could see everything he threw before it was coming. I was totally alert and ready to make him pay.

CHAPTER 18
THE YOUNG LIONS

若獅子

On my second day in the dormitory I had my head shaved, as was the *uchi deshi* tradition. The first time an *uchi deshi* had his head shaved, they had a local barber do it, but after that the guys just cut each other's hair with clippers in the dorm. I looked in the mirror at my new haircut, and already I 'couldn't recognize the person I used to be.

I was now a real *uchi deshi*.

We only had each other to depend on in this mercilessly tough and rigorous environment, and there were some unique personalities among us I'll remember for life. Think about the sort of character who decides to give up everything for karate, leaving their hometown and family to spend three years in a dormitory, trying to graduate from one of the toughest courses in the world.

The first-year sleeping quarters was extremely compact, so you really had to get along with your fellow *uchi deshi* in order to survive. The conditions were incredibly spartan and it was far from comfortable until you got used to it. In the first-year quarters, there were six single Japanese-style futons pressed together on each side of the room for us to sleep on.

Our group of first-year *uchi deshi* only got one creaky and rusted old fan to share between us. The fan rotated so slowly that by the time it came back to me ten seconds later, I was covered in sweat again. It reminded me way too much of the opening scene of the movie *Apocalypse Now*, one of my favorite movies as a teenager. In that scene, Martin Sheen is lying on his bed with a ceiling fan rotating above him that sound like the blades of a helicopter, as he sweats in agony. The oppressive heat of Asia looked terrible on the silver screen, but now that I was feeling it, it was even worse – and I didn't even have a ceiling helicopter, er, I mean fan. I wished I 'hadn't watched *Apocalypse Now* before moving to Japan!

Some guys tried to deal with the heat by sleeping right under the window to catch any breeze. But when the windows were open, mosquitos swarmed in and devoured us. The weird thing was that they usually attacked the new guys the most, and you got bit less and less the longer you'd been there.

No matter what, we'd sweat constantly, and when I slept right on the tatami mats because they were cooler, I'd practically have to peel myself off the tatami in the morning. Looking back, I guess it was probably designed that way to toughen us up.

Luckily, no one snored in our sleeping quarters, but some of the Japanese used to talk in their sleep, especially Kato (a first-year *uchi deshi*). Kato would mumble on for 30 seconds at a time in bits and pieces. I never could make out what he was rambling on about, but the other Japanese *uchi deshi* seemed really concerned. Even Yamakagi was horrified by what was coming out of Kato's mouth in his sleep, and nothing ever fazed Yamakagi. He must have been saying some really crazy stuff!

I didn't snore, either, but I did grind my teeth in my sleep – a bad habit I still have to this day. Sometimes, my teeth grinding was so loud that it woke me up, so I wonder if I pissed off the Japanese in the room.

But not everyone realized the noises were coming from me grinding my teeth. After about six months of living there, one of my dorm mates confessed that he'd thought there were rats in the ceiling making all that noise until he finally realized it was me! Looking back, it was amazing so many people from all over the world got along.

Allow me to introduce some of the other *uchi deshi* who would live and train by my side. Do you remember that bar scene from *Star Wars*, with aliens of all shapes and sizes from all corners of the galaxy? That's what the Young Lions dormitory looked like to me, except there were more dangerous characters in the dojo than in that bar.

Mohamad (who the Japanese called Mokodomo, because they couldn't pronounce his name) was Algerian French. He was the first foreigner accepted as an *uchi deshi* when he had only been 17 years old, while most *uchi deshi* were 18 or 19. He was very intelligent, speaking English, French, and even fluent Japanese. Mohamad pretty much kept to himself, and was a fantastically gifted technician. He didn't have great power, but his technique was superb, and he would pick up new things effortlessly. However, sometimes he would cruise, trying to get by on his incredible natural athleticism alone, and that proved to be his downfall later on.

Mohamad had his own fan because he was a second-year, and with that came privileges. I used to sit next to him and start up a conversation, or find any excuse at all just to feel some of the cool breeze from his fan. Thanks to our many chats, his English became pretty good, and I even picked up a few words of French, all because of that fan!

Yamakagi was the Japanese student I was closest to. We became great mates and brothers in arms. Yamakagi was the same year as me, and his nickname was the Pink Panther because he was such a smooth character. He was skilled, very strong both physically and mentally, and a real cool cat. Being so talented, along with his confidence and "nothing fazes me" personality, he could really do what he pleased. However, this only became evident in his second and third year when he was a senior. When he was a first-year, he was a robot like the rest of us, a foot soldier at the beck and call of the seniors. When I say robot, I don't mean it as a negative; that's what you had to be to survive. The seniors were the ones with the power. They told us what to do and we deferred to them on everything. If you think drill sergeants are bad in the military, the Young Lions dojo was on another level altogether.

The Pink Panther was one of those guys who took everything in his stride. He had an oak-like resilience. As a first-year he was skinny, but already very strong. He did as he was told, but he had an incredibly strong spirit and he didn't take guff from anyone. The Pink Panther had an incredible sense of humor and a wry smile, and in our first year his funny bone served him well, since things were so tough for us. We had fun, but he still managed to keep his personality low-key in the first year out of respect. You always had to be on the lookout for your seniors and be obedient at all times.

Slacking off or cracking jokes was frowned upon, and a good reason to get punched square in the chest by an older student. As a first-year, you constantly had your guard up, alert, and were at the beck and call of all the second- and third-year students. It was like being a private in the army – probably worse, actually. You could cop a verbal bashing at any stage, and if you didn't smarten up, you would get the physical bashing in the dojo.

Nick Pettas arrived in my second year as an *uchi deshi*, in 1991, but I'll talk about him now, as he was very important to me, ultimately becoming my best friend in the dojo. Nick had enrolled as a first-year *uchi deshi* coming from Denmark. He was a young, fresh-faced, eager kid, very skinny, and I used to joke about it, calling him "Broomstick" because he was so thin. He was a good-natured kid, he spoke great English, had a vibrant sense of humor, and we got along really well.

Since day-to-day life was so physically and mentally monotonous for us, and we foreigners were always *gaijin,* or outsiders, to the Japanese, it was a relief to have another outsider who was going to be there for three years on the same mission as we were. Later on, I also found out that Nick's father had died when he was a baby, so perhaps we also had a connection there – both growing up without fathers. Nick, like me, also says to this day that Sosai Mas Oyama was like his father.

Nick was already a brown belt first *kyu* (one level under black belt) when he arrived, and he had great skill and technique. He was one of the highest kickers I had ever seen,

The Young Lions

and his attitude toward training was great. He would always train extremely hard. He wasn't strong at the start, because he was so skinny, but he had great determination. Anyway, when he came in 1991, I was very pleased to have him on board and to join us on our mission. By second and third year, Nick, the Pink Panther and I were inseparable.

During my first year in the dojo, the person I related to most was Nathan Ligo, who slept on the futon beside me for one and a half years. He was from North Carolina and had a non-Kyokushin background. His teacher, who was also Korean, was friends with Sosai from way back, so he had asked if his gifted student could be an *uchi deshi*.

Ligo had great flexibility and sharp high kicks, although his punches weren't good, and his general power wasn't as strong as those coming from a Kyokushin Karate background. But what we both definitely had in common was a love of karate and training and, more than anything else, we were the only two native English speakers in the entire dojo. So Ligo was really the only guy I could speak to in the first year.

Ligo and I shared a love of music and both owned big yellow Sony Walkmans, so we would swap tapes and listen to them at night. We listened to the Yokosuka Base radio station, too, as the Iraq War was going on at that time, and it was the only station in Japan broadcasting in English and playing western music, so we took what we could get. I found out that we both had left our girlfriends behind, so Ligo and I had that in common, too.

From the beginning, Ligo had a loud, affable Hollywood moxie that made him fun to be around, but proved an ill fit when it came to the rules and structure of a Japanese dojo. He seemed to be set in his ways, and refused to change. There was no doubt he was incredibly intelligent, as he could speak English, French, and Korean, and learned to read and write *hiragana* and *katakana*. He was also enthusiastic, had good technique, trained hard, and helped direct me a great deal in the beginning. We got along well, which was convenient since we

THE YOUNG LIONS

were the only two native English-speaking foreigners during my first year. I liked Ligo and we spent a lot of time together, and it wasn't until later that his American swagger began to cause him trouble.

Sandor was from Hungary, and I thought of him as some sort of Hungarian Hulk. He was full on and one of the strongest guys in the dojo, and never took guff or bullying from anyone. Sandor arrived at the same time as me, and was called an *uchi deshi* even though he was staying for only four months.

Technically *uchi deshi* translates directly as "live-in student," no matter how long they stayed. Many people over the years have come over to Japan and called themselves *uchi deshi*, and there has been some controversy about this, but in reality they are correct. If you were invited and came to live and train inside the *Honbu*, you were an *uchi deshi*. The difference is that, to be considered one of Sosai's Young Lions, you had to be invited to train for the full 1,000 days.

Matsui Senpai was a senior teacher at the *Honbu*, and Sosai's right-hand man. He was a serious guy, and also Korean-Japanese like Sosai. Matsui was a world champion fighter, a master tactician, and in 1987 he won the World Open Weight Championship and completed the 100-man *kumite* in the same year. So, to have him as one of the key *Honbu* teachers was just incredible. He was diplomatic and fair to all, both the Japanese and foreigners, and as I improved, we gained a mutual respect for each other – although he always remained private and reserved, never opening up to you like your mates do back home. He was a nice guy; he just never let people get too close.

Being Sosai's number one guy, he delivered messages to the *uchi deshi* that came down from Sosai, telling them where they needed to improve and pick up the pace. Matsui was a good guy, all in all, and a legend in the sport, making it a a privilege to learn from him.

Kuruda was another who began during the same year as me. He was one of the nicest *uchi deshi*, but as sweet as he was off the mats, he was equally a complete machine in the dojo. He trained like a wild animal, following every task 100% as told, always technically correct, and Kuruda would also help anyone. Very different from Pink Panther, you knew Kuruda would never go down the path of the dark side. He was respectful to everyone, he always tried to look out for me – even though in the beginning I didn't speak any Japanese – and I was appreciative of his efforts. He was the epitome of the perfect *uchi deshi*, the perfect foot soldier. He would take all orders, yell *osu* at every instruction, and sprint from place to place as expected. He was what you might call the poster boy of all the *uchi deshi*.

But not everyone in the dojo was so agreeable. Yui Senpai was a former *uchi deshi* who had stayed on at the *Honbu* as a teacher. Yui was about 5'7", 180 pounds (82 kg), and very muscular. As an *uchi deshi,* he was actually one year under Wada Sensei. When I first arrived, he was about 25 and had been teaching there since he graduated – about three years. From the outset, he made it clear he didn't like me, Ligo, or, later on, Nick. Then again, he didn't even like the Japanese students. In fact, Yui Senpai didn't seem to like anyone. He was a complete hard-ass – mean to the core, angry, and never had anything nice to say to anyone.

Yui was also a very cruel person. If anyone was the bully of the dojo, it was Yui Senpai. He used to dole out all sorts of punishment to the *uchi deshi*, especially the first years. He would stare them up and down and say "*Omai*," which is the most impolite and derogatory way of referring to someone in Japanese. He doled out plenty of physical abuse, but he felt the need to heap mental torture on them, too, by making them feel weak, insecure, and helpless. Yui really got into the heads of the Japanese, but we foreigners weren't falling for it. Later on, Nick and I nicknamed him The Ranger, because he would act as judge, jury, and executioner as the unofficial, self-appointed cop of the dojo.

There was Ishida Senpai, who we nicknamed The Barber, because of his terrible haircut that looked like Ringo Starr of

The Beatles.

Then there was Suzuki; a real hardcore Japanese. He was very strict. I'd heard he'd spent time in the Japanese army, and you could easily say we didn't click from the beginning. He was tall for a Japanese – about six feet tall and very wiry – and obedient to Sosai and his seniors, but very bossy even to his equals, and especially with the foreign students. He seemed to have a chip on his shoulder, and he gave the impression that he didn't approve of us foreigners. He was the same year as me, but always pushy, leaving no doubt that he thought he was the boss.

He always had a lot of errands to run that we, as foreigners, didn't have to do because of our imperfect Japanese (at least in the beginning). Maybe he didn't think that was fair, but we also trained harder than he did, so in my eyes we were even. I considered him a rival, because it was obvious that he held animosity towards me, and that came to a head a number of times during my stay in Japan.

Rounding out some of the other *uchi deshi*, who I remember in the beginning, were three other first-years: Ishida, Kato, who I remember was from Kyoto and another great foot soldier; Kumokai; and Hashimoto, a second-year like Mohamad, and the only one staying in the large room upstairs (the other second-years chose to stay on in the larger first-year room).

Then there were the third-years: Yasuyuki Ishiguro and Hamada, the only third-year students when I first started, and both lived in the room on the first floor.

As a first year *uchi deshi*, I didn't interact with those third-year students much, other than to take orders and stand up and bow and shout when they entered a room. But no matter where you were from, what language you spoke, or how long you'd been training at Kyokushin, we all spoke with our fists when it came to the dojo.

CHAPTER 19
BAPTISM BY FIRE

若獅子

The day after I arrived I had my head shaved, as is the *uchi deshi* tradition. I was then told to rest for two days, as that was also an *uchi deshi* rule in order to acclimatize and get over my jet lag and dehydration before beginning the hardest training of my life. But even with two days of rest, when training began it was like being thrown into a pit of hungry wolves.

The very first class I took was Sosai's Thursday class from 1 to 3 PM, which was reserved only for the *uchi deshi*. As you can imagine, I was nervous and jumping out of my skin, wondering what was going to happen and which of the other fighting machines I was going to have to spar. I didn't know what to expect. My heart was racing, my adrenaline pumping, and I was sweating even before the class began.

I put on a white belt like all the other first-years and stepped into formation on the wooden dojo floor. The *Honbu* dojo wasn't a huge space – it could probably have taken 50 students comfortably, or more packed in shoulder to shoulder. On one side there was a traditional Japanese shrine, and on the other all the equipment such as bags, guards, and mitts. There were many pictures of Sosai from all around the world, and some of his more famous students and branch chiefs on the walls. Everything about this place was old school Japanese. The *Honbu* was built in 1964 when Kyokushin was founded, and it looked like it had barely changed in 25 years. With its incense, sacrificial sake and ornaments, the dojo's rich wooden floors and walls, paper sliding doors and windows, and a large Japanese *taiko*, or drum, in the corner, it was just how I had imagined it in my dreams all of those years back in Australia.

Sosai standing directly in front of me was a surreal feeling. Sosai began the count loudly. I punched and kicked to my best ability. I could feel his eyes, now and then, gazing on me, checking to see if I was doing the techniques correctly. I tried to kick as high and strongly as possible *kiai*-ing loud with every move. Sosai stopped in between combinations. Sweat was pouring off his forehead. He looked at me and said, "Don't look down; look straight ahead. Gaze your eyes at the enemy. Your enemy is not a god. He is scared, too. You must focus and don't lose sight of him. Never look away."

I replied with a loud *osu*. I was tired. I took a deep breath. I looked straight ahead. The whole class roared with the sound of loud *kiai'*s.

This first class was almost completely made up of basics and kata, with a lot of practicing of all the kicks, blocks, and punches I had perfected under Wada Sensei in those years at Eddie' Shihan's dojo. It felt comforting to do the familiar movements and forms, my first real refuge from everything that was so new for me since I'd arrived.

At the end of the training session Sosai came over to me and said, "You're from Shihan Eddie's dojo, are you not? You're not a white belt, you're actually a black belt, aren't you?" I hesitantly said yes, not sure exactly how to answer. He then said, "Well, you will wear your black belt from now on." I was both shocked and honored at the same time. All the *uchi deshi*, when they began the course, were made to begin again as white belts, no matter what their previous rank was.

Perhaps Sosai saw my technique, which his very own *uchi deshi*, Wada, had honed with thousands of hours of practice. I may not have been that strong, but Wada Sensei had made sure that my technique was razor sharp. I didn't realize it then, but in the beginning this honor would be a double-edged sword. Being an immediate black belt meant I was going to have to spar with all the black belts in every class, and take all the additional classes only for black belts – which were held on Friday through Sunday. I was the only first-year doing these classes, and the youngest, too. Little did I know what was in store for me in the next few days. When the class was over and Sosai went up to the stairs to his office, I remember he turned and gave me a nod that I felt meant *good job* or *well done*. That simple nod meant the world to me, and I vowed never to let him down.

But those first four days of training, I got completely smashed by it all, especially when I sparred Sandor from Hungary, and he and I went at each other 100%. He was stronger than me at the time, but I hung in there and he didn't drop me. My body was so banged up I couldn't bend my legs at all, and I remember walking up the steep stairs of the dormitory like a mannequin. I had to walk around on my toes because my feet were numb from hopping on the balls of my feet during training, and when I had to squat down to use the traditional Japanese toilet it was pure agony.

But being an *uchi deshi*, you were never to show weakness or complain to anyone. When your *Senpais* asked you how you were doing, you always answered *I'm OK*, no matter what condition you were in. If you failed to block a head kick that rattled your jaw and left you seeing spots, you just steadied yourself and soldiered on. If you got knocked out cold during sparring, the other Japanese students would just sit you up and make sure you were awake, and then you were expected to get back up and keep going. When we started training each morning, my legs would shake, and I couldn't stop the muscles spasms unless I held them. I'm sure the others were the same.

My legs were so bashed up and shocked the first few months that I could barely make it up and down the steep steps of the dojo. They would be as stiff as wood when I woke up, but I had to get up and down the steep stairs to our room. Trying not to let others see me, I would slide down the wall, holding onto the railing so I 'wouldn't gain too much speed and go crashing down. I imagined the humiliation of breaking my leg from something as ridiculous as falling down the stairs!

Even squatting down to use the Japanese toilet was

excruciating, and I almost fell many times when my legs gave out. I thought the pain would last forever, but my body started to adjust and my legs stopped shaking after about three months. The training turned you into a machine; otherwise, you wouldn't survive. Whether it was the resilience of youth or my steadfast obsession with completing Sosai's program, my body recovered quickly and I managed to keep going and always do what was asked of me. But that first week truly tested my resolve.

In the weeks after that, Sandor was a big rival and he would always go as hard as he could with me. He had the upper hand, being bigger and older than me, and he was a world-class fighter. He was not a bad guy. He was just there to train as hard as he could, and that included everything from running the fastest up the hills during sprints, trying to perfect his technique, and sparring as hard as he could. I remember him going hard and really bashing me in the sparring, and today I thank him for this, as it was a big turning point in my training where I had to suck it up and turn up my own training to stay in the game. You either lie down and give up, or you suck it up and improve. You need to go through that punishment to condition not just your body but your mind as well. The mental side is the most important, and if you can get through this type of thing, you can get through anything. "To be a champion fighter, you need to go through that, you need to get bashed," I always thought.

So whenever I sparred Sandor or the other Japanese seniors, I fought like my life depended on it. I went into these sessions with the mindset that there was no way they were going to beat me, unless they carried me out on a stretcher. There was no doubt, no cloudiness; I battled with all my heart and determination. Guys liked Sandor could see this, and tried their best to knock me out. If I made one error against him, let up for one minute, or had any lapse in concentration, it was game over; I'd wake up in the hospital. He was so powerful and explosive, so I had to keep my hands high at all times to block his shots, but even when I deflected his punches and kicks, my forearms were bruised down to the bone. So it was a great feeling when I fought Sandor or the Japanese seniors and held my own, and sometimes even had them on the back pedal.

I'd heard Sandor had been in the Hungarian army before, and he seemed to be the strongest in the dojo by far, at that stage. Although he was only there for four months at the start of my career as an *uchi deshi*, he left a huge impression as a real hard-ass. I wish he had been able to stay with us longer, as I really looked up to him. Sandor had fought in the 1991 World Championship, where in the third round he beat a famous Japanese lightweight fighter called Miyaki. That was a huge upset, and by no means the last of Sandor's accomplishments. He went on to form his own Kyokushin organization, and runs huge international tournaments that focus on developing youth.

Sandor didn't back down from anyone, ever, and that included his seniors and bullies like The Ranger and The Barber. I remember one time they were sparring in class, punching and kicking each other with increasing ferocity. The Barber, always the cruel instigator, tried to push Sandor back into the small shrine that sat in the back of the dojo. Sandor didn't appreciate that slight, and completely lost his temper.

He hurled a thunderous straight right punch that landed squarely on The Barber's head, knocking him to the ground. Sandor moved in over him and was about to unleash a fury of punches to finish the job, but The Ranger grabbed him hard around the neck and pulled him back and told him to stop before he could do so. Sandor was wide-eyed with fury and they were broken up, but there was no further hubbub or reprimands because that kind of thing happened during training.

What the hell was The Barber thinking?

Sandor was such a spirited and strong fighter that he sometimes upset the order of things. I remember in morning training he once knocked a third-year *uchi deshi* down, which was a big no-no by the rules of etiquette. The third-year senior had punched Sandor in the face during training. Rules, of course, dictated that kicks to the head were acceptable, but we could only punch below the neck. I think the senior must have hit him in the face on purpose, because the students all had incredible control and precision by that point.

Well, it was a big mistake to piss off the Hungarian Hulk! Sandor came back with a jet-fast punch that smashed into his senior's face with a boulder-like fist, and the third-year student crumpled to the ground.

Sandor knew instantly the gravity of what he'd just done, but he certainly didn't regret it, as he wasn't one to take any crap from any bully. He thought for sure he'd be thrown out of the Young Lions program for that grave infraction. But Sosai, in his ultimate wisdom, actually threw out the third-year student, and commended Sandor secretly to his staff for sticking up for himself. Our master was never one to put rules ahead of human beings, and embraced the underdog mentality. He wanted to see that fire in his students, and he definitely got a five-alarm blaze with Sandor!

Getting smashed by Sandor wasn't the only thing that made my transition into Japanese life difficult. When I first arrived in the dormitory, the tatami mats were old and frayed, and one morning about two months into my stay I remember waking up with bites all over me, looking like I'd contracted the plague. At breakfast when we were singing the Young Lions song I almost fainted, and I remember getting taken to hospital and having a drip put in my arm. Because of this, the decision came down that the tatami mats were to be replaced, which made life a lot more comfortable.

The strange and sometimes foul-tasting Japanese food also played havoc with me in the beginning, and I almost immediately lost the weight my big, invincible mate Anton had spent a year packing onto my small frame. So after two months I was black and blue with bruises, I could barely walk, my weight had dropped back from 155 (70 kg) to 143 pounds (65 kg), and I was on a drip in a Japanese hospital. Not the successful start I'd hoped for.

Still, I knew it was all part of the process of making me stronger, and if it took going through hell to turn me into a warrior, hell is what I got.

CHAPTER 20
HARDSHIPS OF BEING A FIRST-YEAR UCHI DESHI

若獅子

As a first-year *uchi deshi* you were the lowest of the low. You had no rights, and had to obey your *Senpais*, or seniors', orders no matter what. It was like a military training camp for wannabe karate champions. You were at the beck and call of your *Senpais* 24 hours a day, seven days a week. There were nine of us first-years – so only nine exhausted and shell-shocked bodies to do all the worst jobs, as dished out by the second-years, third-years, and senior instructors at the *Honbu* dojo.

But what the seniors really wanted out of us was discipline and obedience, so they'd push us as hard as they could, to make us physically and mentally as tough as nails – or break us trying. The theory behind our treatment was more than just cruelty. It was about developing character and mental toughness, but with that came a constant element of bullying.

The relationship amongst the *uchi deshi* basically mirrored the Japanese dynamic of *Senpai-kohai*, or "senior and junior." It exists through all of Japanese society, from schools to sports teams to companies – and even to everyday neighborhood relationships – but in the dojo it was taken to a completely different level.

As a *kohai*, or junior, your eyes had to be always watching your seniors to see if they needed something. This is probably the most difficult concept for westerners to understand, because their expectations of a boss or senior is that if they want something done they will get a tap on the shoulder and perhaps a quick "excuse me, can you do such and such?" In Japan, however, if your senior even has to catch your attention, you are already in hot water. Not paying attention to your seniors' every move, and even not being able to recognize his body language, is a sign of laziness and disobedience.

For example, if a *Senpai* was walking toward the entrance of the *Honbu* with a bag, you were automatically supposed to run up to him, take his bag for him, and bring it inside – unless he said *daijobu* ("no, I'm OK").

And when your senior entered the dojo or dormitory, and he casually flicked his shoes off and left them at the door, it was up to the juniors to then run over and turn the shoes around, so that when the senior left, putting on his shoes would be easier.

I remember, in my first year, we were all sitting down in the dining room having breakfast one morning when out the corner of my eye I saw a ceramic bowl go flying across the room and hit one of the first-year Japanese students smack in the head. The senior was yelling things in Japanese that, at that stage, I was still struggling to understand, but I immediately knew the reason why he was angry. The first-year was obviously not paying attention when the senior had finished his rice, and had not asked if he wanted more, so this was his punishment. I remember the junior running over to get a new bowl, and then running over to the rice cooker to fill it up again.

These were the unspoken rules of the *kohai-Senpai* relationship that only someone who has lived amongst it can really understand. This was what was so hard for the first-years. If you didn't like this, understand the Japanese mentality, or adapt to this structure, you were gone.

I remember my hands were all bruised, my knuckles all raw and roughed up and bleeding nonstop. Just when the skin on my knuckles would scab up and be almost healed, they'd rip open again. Even eating meals with my battered hands was a painful affair, but Japanese eating customs (or at least *uchi deshi* customs) made it slightly easier. I'd hold the bowl steady with my left hand and bring it up to my open mouth, and then shovel the food in with a pair of chopsticks held in my right. It worked beautifully because my fingers were too sore to pick things up with chopsticks. To this day, I still eat like this sometimes, and when I'm in a restaurant I always get funny looks from westerners, who think I'm some sort of barbarian.

Letter writing was another adventure with smashed hands. I could forget about writing a letter after a tough training session, as my hands shook uncontrollably and sweat dripped off my hands in the sweatbox dormitory in summer time. Trying to steady the tiny pen, my hand spasms would produce little more than a scribble, and the page was usually streaked in blood from my knuckles by the time I finished. I'd hold up the letter when I was done: soggy with sweat, bloody, and written in a childlike chicken scratch that looked like a 5-year-old wrote it. I couldn't send this to my mum!

The letter would have to wait, and I'd try again later. But even after a cold shower and a few hours to rest, my body didn't cool down; I'd still be sweating, and my knuckles bleeding more than ever. There was no escaping the jungle-like temperatures – and the constant punishment that turned my knuckles into bloody meat.

Some of things we were expected do to as first-years included:

- Scrub the floors, ceilings, walls and every other part of the entire dojo to be absolutely spotless;
- Always be on duty and guard the front of the dojo;
- Clean (and keep spotless) the two toilets in the basement;
- Serve seniors constantly, whether following verbal or instinctive orders;
- Run after any teachers present, and be at their beck and call;
- Wash in one big shower room in the basement with four faucets, and no doors or privacy;
- Wash our clothes in a bucket out front using a single tap, and hang them all out by hand.

Only second- and third-years could use the washing machine, as Sosai Oyama said even the action of washing the *gi* hard with your own hands would make you stronger. I remember when I washed my *gi* in the middle of winter it would freeze up by the time I hung it on the wall and start scrubbing hard. So most of the time during the winter, I'd start training with a stiff and partially frozen *gi*. We had three *gis* and we'd go through at least two a day, as they would eventually be soaking wet with sweat – and, sometimes, stained with blood.

We didn't even wear underwear under our *gi*, and for training we never wore underwear at all, because it looked bad hanging outside with our uniforms. I remember, even years later in Sweden, people looking at me strangely when I wasn't wearing underwear in the change rooms. Second- and third-year students could use the washing machine, and as first-years we had to wash the seniors' *gi* in the washing machine – even though we couldn't use it ourselves.

Even sleeping in the dormitory at the back of the dojo was full of constant reverberating noise. Action was almost never-ending at the dojo, all day, from the first training session in the park at 6 AM to the last class finishing at 9 PM, so the noise was absolutely relentless.

The first-year *uchi deshi* were not even allowed to leave the dojo unless accompanied by one of their *Senpai* or senior students on official Kyokushin business. As well as training three times a day for up to two hours each time, we were expected take turns standing guard at the front of the dojo, cleaning the dojo, and taking orders from our *Senpai*.

Amongst the *uchi deshi*, the attrition rate was high. Every few months the live-in students would wake up one morning and find that one of their colleagues had fled. They always packed their things and snuck out in the middle of the night when they quit, to avoid the shame of failing. Japanese do not like confrontation, so there would be no goodbyes, as the loss of face was too embarrassing. Most of them would never do karate again in their lives.

Hardships of Being a First-Year Uchi Deshi

The training was often brutal, especially the mental side. When I look back now at pictures of us, I can't believe how skinny and naive we were – or maybe it was the fearlessness of youth. Even at the time, I knew I needed to beef up, but the shock of coming over to a country with strange food and oppressive heat made me drop back from 155 pounds (70 kg) to 145 pounds (66 kg) in the first three months. Being away from home couldn't have been easy for the other kids in the dormitory, either, and our spirits would have been crushed if our hearts weren't 100% in the program. But Kyokushin Karate founder Sosai Oyama was a martial arts legend, and to train under him and, hopefully, one day graduate as one of his Young Lions was every karate kid's dream.

When, exactly, this 1,000-day Young Lions course officially started is hard to say. It has been lost somewhat in Japanese Kyokushin folklore, but I'm assuming it began sometime in the early 1980s. The earliest three-year *uchi deshi* I can think of was Takeyama, who graduated perhaps three years before Wada Sensei. But in later years, it came to replicate Sosai Mas Oyama's 1,000 days of training in the mountains, where he developed Kyokushin Karate. So that was the same time period chosen for his *uchi deshi* to graduate: 1,000 days – or, more precisely, three years of training. Sosai called it "1,000 days for the beginning."

These three years were brutal, with incredibly hard conditions and training, so the fallout rate was sometimes as high as 80%, with only 20% of the initial number of students still there at graduation three years later. For that reason, many referred to it as a modern-day gladiator school.

Foreigners from all around the world had come at various times to stay for a single month or up to three months to train. While they were there, they were embedded with us full-time *uchi deshi*. I guess the biggest difference was only that we were referred to as the Young Lions, and we never left the dormitory. (The dormitory itself was actually named the *Wakjishiryo,* meaning "the Young Lions Dormitory.")

Even though there was servitude and tormenting within the

ranks of Young Lions, we were well respected by the other visitors and karate students in the dojo. For instance, even if a visitor was a black belt, the second- and third-year *uchi deshi* were always their seniors in the hierarchy of the dormitory. But we welcomed the visitors, because it was great fun to have someone new to talk to.

While what you read here may at times seem gratuitous and even cruel, I can assure you that the hardships and challenges I faced during my time as an *uchi deshi* turned me into the person I am today.

"Studying the martial Way is like climbing a cliff: keep going forward without rest. Resting is not permissible because it causes recessions to old adages of achievement. Persevering day in, day out improves techniques, but resting one day causes lapses. This must be prevented." –Sosai Oyama

CHAPTER 21
100-MAN KUMITE, FIGHTS 10 THROUGH 30

若獅子

I breezed through the first ten fights. I was just warming up, and feeling on top of the world. I didn't even care about checking or blocking thigh kicks or punches. My body was too strong, and I was working my angles well. I didn't take a single step back, and instead kept moving forward, always the aggressor. When I had to, I shifted quickly to the side, countering everything they threw at me. If they kicked high, I would sweep their bottom leg out from underneath them. If they tried to punch me out, I'd work my angles and they would come out the worse. I was totally in control and dominating each fight.

Nick was giving me sound advice from the corner, and I had an ear out for everything he was saying. I wasn't wearing any shin guards or wraps on my hands, so they must have felt my thigh kicks and punches. Some of the other fighters wore shin guards and mitts, but at the end of the day it's the guy fighting off 100 opponents who's really smashing himself up.

From about the 20th fight on, I started attacking strategically, trying to dispatch my opponents efficiently to conserve energy. As I squared up with one eager black belt after another, I carefully tracked them, anticipating what they were going to do.

When I put pressure on them, the fighters tried to muscle me back. I guess they were just as filled with adrenaline as I was. Taking advantage of their over-aggressiveness, I would quickly take a few steps back, relaxed and composed. As the fighter inevitably charged towards me to fill the void, I would whip a roundhouse kick into their midsection, exactly at the same time they lunged forward with a punch.

It was perfect counter fighting: I'd set them up by letting them throw the first attack, and then I'd counter hard and fast at their weakest point, making them pay every time. The force of them charging squarely into my strongest kick was like two cars having a head-on collision – except that, in the end, they would always be much worse off.

CHAPTER 22
LIFE IN THE HONBU

若獅子

"If someone asked me what a human being ought to devote the maximum of his life to, I would answer: training. Train more than you sleep." –Sosai Oyama

Living full-time in the dormitory for 1,000 days, from the age of 19 to 22; learning not only karate, but also a new language, culture, and hierarchy; and being away from all of my family and childhood friends was tough going for me at times, and it must have been tough for mum and Peter, too. I could receive calls from my family once every three months or so, just to say hi, and only in my second or third year could I call out from the *Honbu*. In my first year, I cherished getting a long letter from my mum with news from back home. When I had the chance, I would send home photos and letters, often showing the lighter side of things. One letter I wrote went like this:

Hi mum,
    I am really enjoying life in Japan. Time is going quickly. Days go long, but weeks go fast. Basically, I train 5 - 6 hours a day. It's very difficult to explain what life is like here. There's a lot of obedience that goes on. "*Osu Osu*" – all the time.
    For example, everything has to be precise. If they say we eat at 8.00, we'll eat at 8.00, and if someone is late, they'll get jumping squats for punishment or scolded, so sometimes it's a little bit rough. The Japanese first-year students are treated like rubbish. They are busy doing

business and running around all the time.

As you can see in the group photos of *uchi deshi's* there are a lot of foreigners – five, to be exact. Only a few of them are here for a short period of time. Don't I look small? I was 65 kg. This photo was taken around summer time and training was extremely difficult. This was the hardest time for me. Every day I felt tired and worn out. Anyway, things have changed since then.

I'll write again soon. Take care, and thank you for the package and money.

Love,

Judd.

Plenty of friends and family back home sent me letters,, and I appreciated every one of them. But day-by-day, the sense of my past life in Australia started fading, until that seemed like a dream but my life in Japan was the reality. My friends talked about doing the typical things that 20-year-olds do, like going to university or getting jobs, going to the discos on the weekends to get drunk, and chasing girls or even thinking about getting married. But what they wrote about all seemed so distant to me. I don't know how else to describe it, but the things they found so important in their lives seemed a little small. I don't mean that in a bad way, but like anything in life we see it through a different perspective once we've moved on.

Instead of the workweek, dating and discos, a typical week in the life of an *uchi deshi* went something like this:

From Monday to Sunday, we would wake up at 5:45 AM. For the first six months, I remember feeling constantly tired. I would wake up having slept very little because of the intolerable heat, humidity and noise, feeling drained, and my heart already beating fast. On top of this, I seemed to be constantly battling injuries such as sore legs and shins, bloodied-up knuckles that never seemed to heal, blistered feet, and a constant build-up of lactic acid.

Every morning, despite our tired state after just waking, we

Life in the Honbu

would go to the park next door and clean up all the rubbish around it and the *Honbu* for 15 minutes. At 6:30 AM, our *Senpais* would come out and we would run up to them, stand in formation, and yell *osu*. Then, in *gi* pants and a white t-shirt, we would be led by the *Senpai* on a run. The run would vary between two to five miles, all around Ikebukuro (the suburb where our dojo was located) depending on the *Senpai*'s mood. Sometimes we would stop at a steep hill in Meijiro and do 10 hill sprints, and then run back to the dojo. We would get back to the stone-paved park around 7 AM.

We'd typically warm up with 100 pushups, sit-ups, and squats, and then do a few rounds of skipping (jump rope). After that, sometimes for creative torture they put us through 1,000 jump squats in a row, a couple hundred pushups until we collapsed, walking handstands on the wood floor of the dojo or concrete park, and then, when we mastered that, walking handstands on our knuckles, or even on our fingertips.

Improving our flexibility was critical, so we would go through painful stretches endlessly, and try to kick a few balls they had hanging from the ceiling at six feet high, seven feet high, and the highest requiring a fighter to kick nine feet in the air. Whenever we mastered the ability to kick one ball, we'd move up to aiming for the next one, and finally we started double kicking them with one jump were brutal on the body, as I would start these marathon morning sessions limping and battered. I remember first waking up in the morning with my heart already beating fast, anticipating the almost round-the-clock exercise I was putting it through. I even had dreams of training, and than woke up exhausted from the dreams.

But, somehow, we had to get up and do it all over again. By that point, we were beyond exhaustion, so it was all mental. Somehow, you had to focus clearly on your goal or else you'd collapse and give up. For me, it became a spiritual pursuit to elevate past the limits of the human body, our loud *kiai*'s echoing through the neighborhood like the prayer bells that rang at Tokyo's Shinto shrines and Buddhist temples.

The park was all concrete – not grass – and I remember as I did my push-ups, fresh blood oozing from my knuckles into the stones and dirt, wondering if my hands would ever heal. (Later on, I could always spot an *uchi deshi* by his scarred, calcified knuckles.) We did so many sit-ups on concrete that the skin on my backside would peel off, and I started doing them a little to the side so the flesh didn't rip off more each time. We would follow that up with shadow boxing, sometimes bringing the bags out and kicking and punching them until about 7:30.

Morning training was mostly focused on increasing our cardio fitness and conditioning. We also did squats with someone on our shoulders for strength, and hit each other in the stomach and chests for conditioning. We worked so hard that there were literally puddles of sweat on the ground around each of us. It made for quite a sight, all of us with shaved heads like a bunch of escaped convicts, soaking wet, our once-white *gi* pants and t-shirts gray and dirt-stained, splotches of blood splattered all over our outfits like a macabre Jackson Pollock painting.

One of the *Senpais* would every now and then yell out to ask what time it was, and one of the *kohai* would yell back, "*Osu,* it's 7:25!" to keep track of time. From 7:30 to 7:45 we would go back to the dorm to change our clothes and relax.

At precisely 8 AM we would meet inside the dining room and read the dormitory rules, or Young Lions Oath (which was different from the *dojo kun*), which basically listed our strict code of Young Lions behavior and the code of ethics in the dormitory. One of the *Senpai* would read each line and then we would repeat it. There were about 10 lines that he would say, and we would repeat each until it was complete, standing in line and at attention facing the front. Then the *Senpai* would press play on a large tape recorder that played the Young Lions song, and we would all sing the *Wakajishiryo Ryoka,* or Young Lions Song, together. Still, to this day, I don't know who that singer on the tape recorder was.

As I said, the First-years would set up the breakfast table

Life in the Honbu

while Robo San would oversee the cooking of the rice, miso soup, egg, nori, and natto. It was the exact same breakfast every day for three years.

From 8:10 to 9:00 I would go to the *Honbu* dojo with the Pink Panther, and our chores were to clean the basement with a rag and make sure the toilets were clean. The seniors each had their own small locker in the basement, and we needed to make sure a towel was folded correctly and placed over the door of their locker, as well as line all their shoes and slippers up perfectly. Everyone had different chores. Some would clean the dojo itself, some would clean the foyer, and some the staircase. Anything that needed to be cleaned in the *Honbu* dojo was spotless at all times.

Eating the same thing every single day was bad enough, but I can't overstress the pure monotony of doing the same chore every day at exactly the same time.

There was a clock near the entrance of the basement, and I used to look at the second hand ticking slowly around. I swear, sometimes it felt like when it got to the bottom number six that it slowed down and was struggling to make it back up to the top. It was just my brain, saying, "Sometimes I wish that clock would hurry up!" I also remember thinking, "Thank god it's not going backwards." I couldn't wait to be a second-year *uchi deshi*, as even though you still had chores, at least it would give me some room to breathe.

At 9:30 AM, we assembled for the meeting with Sosai Mas Oyama, who would deliver our talk for day, called the *chore*. The morning *chore* started with a formality before Sosai addressed us, as we'd line up in formation and a great drum, called a *"taiko,"* would be beaten. Literally translating to "big drum" in Japanese, its origins go back as far as the 6th century CE, and it holds a mythical reverence. It was first used in warfare, to motivate and communicate with troops, and through the centuries has come to be used in traditional Japanese music, theater, small town festivals, and religious ceremonies at shrines.

Our *taiko* sat in the back corner of our dojo by a shrine. It was a beautiful and ornate percussion instrument, handcrafted from a single piece of wood from the trunk of a Japanese zelkova tree, then dried and fitted with a stretched animal hide. The *taiko* was laid horizontally on a small wooden stand and the class instructor would have the honor of beating it with a stick, starting with three sets of four drum beats, representing *ha ji me ru*, which means "start" in Japanese, and then three sets of three drum beats to represent *wa re ru* at the end of class, which means "finished."

The drumming would start off measured but then build faster with each beat, coming to a crescendo with one last loud and powerful note that echoed in the silence of the room as we stood at attention, our heartbeats suddenly matching the *taiko*'s cadence.

I heard those drumbeats at every single class during my 1,000 days..

Sometimes I would be in the dormitory and running a little late for class, for whatever reason, but when I heard that first drumbeat for the morning *chore*, I knew I only had about 30 seconds to make a mad dash up the stairs to the *Honbu* dojo and line up in formation. I just made it every time.

Whenever I walked into the dojo, whether I was exhausted, my body was beat up, or I had my mind on other things, the ritual beating of the drum and kneeling down in *seize* (on my knees) with my eyes closed would instantly clear my mind and help me focus in on what was ahead. *Boom! Boom! Boom-boom!* When I heard those four deep and echoing drum beats, I was at the pinnacle of concentration and nothing could distract me. This is the Budo way, and why traditions are so important in Kyokushin Karate.

We all stoodIn *fudo dachi* formation at attention with our feet together. Sometimes Sosai would be a little late, so we'd stand for five or ten minutes like that. I remember being so fatigued that my body began to sway, like a drunken sailor on deck the morning after a bender. When Sosai then entered the dojo I had

Life in the Honbu

to concentrate in order not to lose my balance. I'm sure the other *uchi deshi* felt the same.

Once Sosai Oyama stepped into the room, all 12 or 13 of us would yell at the top of our lungs *osu!* And he would say *osu* back. The volume of the *osu* was dependent on the level of respect, so even with my eyes closed I could almost pick out to whom the *osu* was directed – and Sosai Oyama always got the loudest *osu* of them all.

Starting at 9:30, for anywhere from five to 30 minutes, Sosai Oyama would talk to us about the day ahead, what he expected from us, and would try to motivate us by telling us what we were lacking and needed to improve upon. He would talk about life and encourage us and preach to us, talk about hardship, tell stories about his experiences, and explain how he overcame adversity. It took a while until my Japanese was good enough to understand everything, but then I loved hearing about Sosai's life, and those talks put me on the right path for the day.

Unfortunately, for the first six to 12 months I understood very little of what he was saying, until I could speak Japanese. I really learnt Japanese by immersion with other Japanese students. I already knew the simple alphabets *hiragana* and *katakana* when I arrived, with their 44 characters each, but I didn't know any *kanji* or complicated Chinese characters – of which there are about 10,000. In fact, you have to know about 3,000 *kanji* just to read the average newspaper. Spoken Japanese, on the other hand, I never really found all that difficult, and with little time for books outside of training, the other Japanese I interacted with on a daily basis were my very effective teachers.

The first class was from 10 AM to noon and was called *ichibu*. That was for everyone – *uchi deshi* and *soto deshi* (outside, or casual student) alike. It was just a general warm-up, with basic drills, kata, fighting and bow off, and always at the end there was the reading of the *Kyokushin Dojo Kun*. The *Kyokushin Dojo Kun*, or Dojo Oath, was written by Sosai Masutatsu Oyama and the famous Japanese writer Eiji Yoshikawa, who was one of his inspirations.

The *Dojo Kun* comprises a list of rules to follow in the dojo, but would also be impactful throughout your entire life. At the end of every training session, the teacher recited the *Dojo Kun* out loud, with each student repeating the words after him while sitting in *seiza*, or kneeling, position. Studying the *Dojo Kun* is an excellent way to try to understand the philosophy of Kyokushin Karate.

For those who are interested, this is the *Kyokushin Karate Dojo Kun*:

Hitotsu, wareware wa, shinshin o renmashi, kakko fubatsu no shingi o kiwameru koto.
We will train our hearts and bodies for a firm unshaken spirit.

Hitotsu, wareware wa, bu no shinzui o kiwame, ki ni hasshi, kan ni bin naru koto.
We will pursue the true meaning of the martial way so that, in time, our senses may be alert.

Hitotsu, wareware wa, shitsujitsu goken o motte, kokki no seishin o kanyo suru koto.
With true vigor, we will seek to cultivate a spirit of self-denial.

Hitotsu, wareware wa, reisetsu o omonji, chojo o keishi, sobo no furumai o tsutsushimu koto.
We will observe the rules of courtesy, respect our superiors, and refrain from violence.

Hitotsu, wareware wa, shinbutsu o totobi, kenjo no bitoku o wasurezaru koto.
We will follow our religious principles and never forget the true virtue of humility.

Hitotsu, wareware wa, chisei to tairyoku to o kojo sase, koto ni

nozonde ayamatazaru koto.
We will look upwards to wisdom and strength, not seeking other desires.

Hitotsu, wareware wa, shogai no shugyo o karate no michi ni tsuji, Kyokushin no michi o mattou suru koto.
All our lives, through the discipline of karate, we will seek to fulfill the true meaning of the Kyokushin way.

After completing the *Dojo Kun,* everyone would file past the instructor say *domo arigato gozaimanshita,* or "thank you very much," and everyone would shake every member's hands with two hands, as is the respectful Japanese custom. Then everyone would grab a small rag and clean the floor three times in a predetermined format, running while doing it.

From noon to 12:30 PM we would shower and get ready for lunch.

Lunch was always at 12:30 but the cuisine would vary, though there would always be rice, meat (either pork, chicken, or fish), and maybe a miso soup and some pickles, and more *mugicha* (cold tea) to drink. Lunch would be devoured in a slightly more leisurely fashion than breakfast – in maybe five to 10 minutes. Sometime your *Senpai* would order you to eat another bowl of rice, and you always said *osu* and *itadakimasu,* and did so without question. Also, the *kohai* would constantly watch the *Senpai's* bowl, and if it began to empty he would ask him if he wanted a refill. This is the way it was.

The job of the *kohai* was to be the *Senpai's* full-time servant, if not his slave. To not act this way was seen as a great sign of disrespect, and not the behavior of a good *uchi deshi.*

From 12:45 to 4 PM was down time, unless you had chores to do. With any down time, guys would also read books, magazines, write letters home, listen to music, or work on the daily writing in our diaries that Sosai required, as he would collect them every day and approve them with a stamp. The *gaijin* didn't have as many chores, mainly because we didn't have the language ability, so we would often use this time to catch up on much-needed rest and sleep. The Japanese, on the other hand, would either do the same or, if their seniors allocated them chores, they would have to do this. The chores included running things to the post office, going to the bank, standing in the lobby to guard it, and answering the phone or guiding visitors to wherever they needed to go.

The class from 4 to 6 PM was called *nibu*. Basically, it was the same class as the 10 AM one, but these afternoon classes were run by senior *uchi deshi* or senior Kyokushin instructors who'd been around for many years. These classes were open to everyone.

Dinner was at 6:30 PM, again for five to 10 minutes. The food was about the same as lunch, but there was more to eat.

The 7 to 9 PM *sanbu* class was always taught by a senior instructor', someone who'd been at the *Honbu* for five to 15 years – perhaps someone like Matsui or Sugimora, who I'll talk about later. This class was more intense, and there was always fighting for the last 30 to 45 minutes. We concentrated on fighting full contact from 30 to 100% intensity, depending on the skill and strength of our opponents.

In this class, black belts from outside of the *uchi deshi* program would turn up for the second half of the class, nice and fresh, specifically for sparring. If you knew you were going to do that class, you would skip dinner at 6:30 and have it at 9:30 PM instead, so you wouldn't throw up. Robo San would leave around 5 PM, but there was always a cooker filled with rice and a lidded pot on the stove filled with some kind of meat.

10 PM was bedtime. There was no specific lights-out, but by this time we were usually so exhausted we'd go straight to sleep, except the first-first year uchi deshi, who were always battling the heat and their banged up bodies.

Thursday was exactly the same, except we had a special class for the first-year *uchi deshi* only, taught by Sosai from 1 to 3 PM. His class was strictly basics and *kata*. Some of the *uchi deshi* came in as white belts, with no previous formal karate training, so this was the class where they perfected their basics.

But, like I said, Sosai singled me out during my very first training session and told me to wear my black belt. Looking back, this must have provoked some jealousy amongst the other *uchi deshi*, as even though I was still a junior, I was now the *Senpai*, in a sense, to many of the other students in the dojo because I was a higher belt than they were. However, in the general scheme of the *uchi deshi* hierarchy, I was still the lowest of the low, being just another first-year.

Friday was the same, except for the *sanbu* from 7 to 9 PM, which was also taught by Sosai, and it was a black-belt-only class. Many people would come in from different dojos to join this class. Since Sosai allowed me to wear my black belt, it meant I was lucky enough to also attend this class, which made me feel very privileged. Friday night was a very technical class with higher *kata*, more technical karate moves, and initially in the first year it was a lot of basics, but I remember in my second and third year Sosai seemed to change his methodology and introduced a lot more sparring for the last 30 to 45 minutes of the class.

On Saturday morning we would wake and warm up, but there was no morning class. There was a 1 to 3 PM class with Sosai, and this was the biggest class of the week, as it was open to everyone of all belts, and sometimes up to 80 or 100 people would squeeze in, shoulder to shoulder. Sometimes people would have to sit down at the back and rotate to get a turn to train. It has been said in the press that in the mid-80s, at the height of Sosai's fame, that dozens of people used to stand out in front on the street to be a part of the class, training on the road at the same time as the class was conducted inside. He was that iconic, like a martial arts rock star. This Saturday class was beginners and intermediate to advanced, and this again was basics, *kata*, and fighting combinations – lots of punching and kicking drills, but no fighting.

The *uchi deshi* didn't do the other classes on Saturday. There was no *ichibu*, and we generally didn't do *nibu* or *sanbu* because we had a weekly dinner with Sosai at 6:30, which was an even bigger event than training with the Master.

The dinner was held in the dormitory with only us *uchi deshi*. This was an absolute feast, something like you might have seen in medieval days. I will talk about this eating frenzy a bit later on, as this was harder than training at times, but I will tell you a story now.

Sosai would often pass plates of food to some of the *uchi deshi* and say, "you need to eat more to get bigger and stronger," and the *uchi deshi* would yell *osu!* and eat more. No one would ever say "no" or "I've had enough." We would always eat more, no matter what. I remember one particular time where Sosai was at the head of the table at a function where there was an assorted plate of sushi on the table, and in the center of this plate was a flower as a decoration. Sosai ordered one of my fellow second-year *uchi deshi*, Kumokai, to eat everything on that plate. We knew Kumokai's character, and he was literally going to eat everything on that plate – so he even ate the flower! Nick, the Pink Panther and I tried to hold in our laughter, but burst out in hysterics – even though Sosai was oblivious to what had happened.

Sunday is usually a holiday in most sports, but for an *uchi deshi* it was one of the toughest days. The training routine was the same: there was *ichibu*, but I usually skipped that class, knowing what was coming after.

On the Sunday there was no *nibu* or even *sanbu*, but there was another black belt class like on Friday – this one from 4 to 6 PM. Again, a lot of Japanese black belts from around Tokyo would come to participate in this class. Attendance may have been about 30 to 50 in this class. But what was interesting about this class was that there were so many famous fighters that I had seen in magazines, who would come specifically for this class. Names included Kimoto, Ishi, Kurojima, and guys who were currently fighting in the biggest tournaments but who had not yet opened their own dojos.

Sosai really pushed the higher grades during those Sunday classes. He would demand 100% effort for every single punch and kick. I think I learnt the most from these classes, with Sosai standing directly in front of us, leading the way.

Sosai's punches were incredible works of athletic artistry that I could watch like others may watch Michael Jordan play basketball or Ronaldo kick a football. Like a cobra striking, I could see him generating power up through his legs, through his hips, up his back, and shooting out through his fists. His whole body was behind the punch, and the sound of his fist ripping through the air made a loud snapping noise, even when he was just shadowboxing. As we lined up in formation, sweat dripping down our faces, and hanging on his every word, Sosai explained that you really get your power from your *chi*, your life force, which generates from your stomach. He'd walk down the line, striking each of us in our abdomen with only two fingers, saying, "Concentrate on getting your power from here. Don't think about getting power from your arms or shoulders."

There was no detail too small for him to drill into us again and again. He clenched his fists tightly, finger by finger, demonstrating how to make a proper fist, and explaining it thoroughly every class. Who would think a simple thing like that would be so important? But there was no denying the result, as his club-like fists looked as if they could stop a charging bull in its tracks.

Sosai was also stunningly flexible. Even at his age, he could drop down into a full split effortlessly. Not age, nor his muscular barrel chest, nor his powerful frame inhibited him from bending and stretching his body like the most practiced yogi. He'd unleash the most spectacular kicks far above his head, as instinctual and smooth as someone else might flick their finger.

He'd been training every day his whole life. I remember reading a magazine, years ago, in which the interviewer asked Sosai what he loved most about karate. His answer was simply that he loved to train! "Don't be surprised if one day I just disappear," he told the journalist, "just so I can be left alone to train."

Those Sunday classes were sure something else. Higher-grade karate fighters from all over Japan would travel hundreds of miles just to attend this class. I treasured these sessions, and the honor of learning directly from Sosai was never lost on me.

It was a very intense class, very technical, with lots of kicking combinations and *kata*. Again, in my first year, I remember there wasn't much fighting, but this too changed in my second and third year. There must have been some sort of change in strategy in Oyama's thinking around that time, because the fighting became a much bigger part of training in my last two years.

Being awarded my black belt from the beginning may have created some dissension amongst the other *uchi deshi*, but in my eyes it didn't make my life easier by any standard. As you can see from the schedule, many of the classes from Thursday through Sunday were for black belts only, and since I was a black belt it was compulsory that I attend these classes – bearing in mind that they were also the toughest classes of the week. I'm not complaining, of course, because training with the best of the best of Kyokushin Karate, and under the founder Sosai Oyama himself, could only rapidly improve me, getting me closer to my goal of one day being World Champion. I was living my dream.

Sosai Oyama ruled with an iron fist. His students obeyed him no matter what. Whatever he told them to do, they would do without hesitation. There was a rumor that he once told a student to immediately leave the dojo in the quickest way possible, so the student went straight to a window of the second floor and jumped out onto the street – injuring himself in the process. I can't confirm this, as it may have been just a myth, but I have to say it wouldn't surprise me if it were true.

In my second year, Nick and I often joked that if Sosai ordered the Japanese *uchi deshi* to come into the dorm and kill us, they would have done so without hesitation. This just gives you an idea of the control and power he held over his students. Thankfully, he never gave that order, though I thought the training would surely do me in at times.

CHAPTER 23
CLASSES WITH SOSAI

若獅子

Sosai taught a special class for the *uchi deshi* every Thursday. What really amazed me about Sosai, at first, was when he taught the classes he was taking the count, doing all of the exercises and forms and leading the way himself. He would always do the stretching, warm-up, and basics, even though he was 68 years old at that time. It was hard enough work for 20-year-olds, so it was remarkable that he insisted on doing this himself, even at more than triple our ages. He would be sweating profusely, his face dripping, and his karate *gi* was soaked with perspiration, but he never wavered. He would always start the class wearing a bandana, and once it was sweat-soaked he would take it off and use it as a kind of towel. He would train the basics non-stop for about an hour, and not once did he stop or show weakness or fatigue. He could have easily gotten one of the younger students to do the count, and just walk around like I see most senior teachers do these days, but not Sosai. He led by example. What a man!

After the *kihon* (basic kicks, punches, and blocks on the spot), Sosai would nominate us to take turns doing the count for the *idogeko* (basic punching and blocking, while walking up and down), and he would walk over to the back of the dojo where there was a bench and some dumbbells, and he would do some basic weight training for about 20 minutes during every *uchi deshi* class. I think the idea was not just that he would get the chance to train or rest, but also give us *uchi deshi* some autonomy and experience in teaching the group.

When he was satisfied with the punching and blocking drills, he would walk back over to the front of the dojo and sit on a cushion on a raised platform next to the shrine. He would then order us to take the count through a series of kicking drills. This would last about 30 minutes. He would sit there, overlooking us and pulling us up if we were doing things incorrectly or not to his satisfaction. By this stage, about 90 minutes had passed, and we'd literally done hundreds of punches and kicks.

He would then stand up and orchestrate us through *kata*. He would walk around the class, correcting our posture and telling us where our power should be coming from. He would break the techniques down and explain how little things could improve our power and speed by a huge percentage. And that was our typical two-hour class with Sosai. Sosai would teach four classes each week, from Thursday through Sunday, right to the very last of his days.

In our first year, our weekly *uchi deshi* class with Sosai was all about getting our technique absolutely perfect. I sometimes wished we could skip past drilling on all of these basics, but through this hard work, we became as agile and balanced as ballet dancers. In other classes, if we did the littlest thing wrong the seniors would whack us on our forearms, legs, or shoulders with a bamboo stick, though Sosai Oyama never had to do this – we were all extra focused and striving for perfection when training with him. Later on, after my first year, it was more about timing, speed, balance, and breathing so we could generate the maximum amount of power out of our kicks and punches in fighting, and I was then very happy we'd spent all of that time getting our technique perfect during my first year.

Sosai Oyama's favorite saying was, "There is no secret to becoming strong, only plenty of sweat and hard training." As he said this, he would wipe the sweat off his face, as if to say, "See? It's no big deal, you just have to try." How can you not respect a man like this? I'm sure he was tired at times, like the rest of us, but his entire focus was to get the best out of us, and he did that by filling us with ambition to push harder and harder.

In the classes, he was very strict but extremely encouraging. It's not that we learnt any special tricks or secret techniques from him, but it was all about the way he taught that made him such a special and gifted teacher. He knew when we were fatigued or exhausted, and he would know exactly when to say encouraging and philosophical things that would reach deep into our spirits and pull that extra strength out of us – strength that we didn't think we had, only moments before. We felt like there were no limits, as long as he was leading us. I had complete faith in everything he said, and we did everything he asked, never questioning him, and never once did I ever doubt him. He had many, many sayings, a lot of which he would repeat over and over in class, and these often come back to me throughout my life, taking on renewed meaning and helping me all over again. I remember one saying he repeated often to us was, "You should train more than you sleep."

There was no room for error in Sosai's classes. When we were practicing techniques, everything had to be executed with 100% effort and accuracy. This was what Sosai demanded from us, all of the time. If we slacked off in the least, he would have no qualms about scolding us. When members of the class were doing the count, if they messed it up he would not hesitate to yell at them, "*Omai bakayaro* – you idiot!" This meant we were always giving it our all, and we were extremely focused on the mental side of training. Looking back, this had to be one of the reasons he produced so many champions. Of course, no one can keep this level of intensity up for an unlimited amount of time, but Sosai had this uncanny intuition, knowing when to pull back and let us rest. And while we rested for maybe 30 seconds to a minute, he would walk up and down the front of the dojo and perhaps correct our stance and posture, or straighten someone's *gi*, and at the same he would tell us, "Don't just concentrate on one thing. You must concentrate equally on power, speed, technique, timing, and breathing. These are the five essential elements you must master in karate."

By the end of Sosai's classes we would be totally exhausted.

Our *gi* would be saturated in sweat, our legs would be shaking, and from our early morning training sessions, blood would still be dripping from our knuckles onto the dojo floor. Every session just seemed to be adding more blisters to my already blistered feet. It was only after about three months of full-time training that my hands and feet began to calcify, and the bleeding and blisters disappeared.

Sosai would tell us young *uchi deshi* that we must train every single day. Every day we trained, we would move forward. If we missed a day, we would go backwards. So the aim was to train several times a day, every day of our lives.

What did the relentlessness of the training feel like? Do you remember the Greek legend of Sisyphus, who was doomed to push a boulder up a hill every day of his life, only to start anew every morning? Or maybe you've seen that part of the movie *Conan the Barbarian*, where Arnold is pushing the wheel around in circles by himself? Well, I'm pretty sure. He broke a lot of people – mentally, I'm sure, but also physically. I often thought of that graffiti on the wall of the dormitory I'd spotted my very first morning, "When the going gets tough, the tough get going." I bet the ones that were left at the end look back at that crazy time fondly, knowing that the Young Lions course forged them forever, helping them smash through whatever challenges they would face the rest of their lives. Even those who just train in Kyokushin Karate, they always say that the training and discipline they learn helps them with their everyday life.

CHAPTER 24
FIGHTING MY HERO, WADA SENSEI

若獅子

"If you have confidence in your own words, aspirations, thoughts, and actions and do your very best, you will have no need to regret the outcome of what you do. Fear and trembling are lot of the person who, while stinting effort, hopes that everything will come out precisely as he wants." –Sosai Oyama

Around September of 1990, Sosai Oyama devised a test to select the *Honbu* fighters for the All Japan Tournament. It involved doing all sorts of push-ups and other exercises for about an hour first, and then we all sat down and Goda Shihan, Sosai's second in charge, set up everyone for a fight that would last for one intense 5-minute round.

About halfway through the match-ups, having watched several fights, my name was called. I went to stand up, but almost fell back down when, to my shock, Wada was named as my opponent. I had been matched up against my hero – the teacher I had idolized and copied for so many years! I'm sure he was just as shocked that he was about to fight his old friend and student – someone so far his junior. This was one of those things in life that you can't foresee; a crazy twist of fate that came crashing at my feet.

So Wada Sensei and I were fighting each other for a place in the All Japan – and only one of us could come out the victor. Wada had returned to training at the *Honbu* regularly for a couple of months before this, with the sole aim of making the All Japan, so this was perhaps even more important to him than it was to me.

I had been training one on one with Wada Sensei to prepare for this fight, though I had no idea I was training him to take me down. But of course I was truly honored for the time he spent with me in the lead-up to this event. After all, he was the reason why I was an *uchi deshi* in the first place, and my hero. I also did a lot of training with an Iranian named Hussein, and he trained very hard, was well respected, and he had placed sixth in the previous year's All Japan, beating Kurosawa and going on an extension with the future World Champion Yamaki Kenji. I have to admit I felt very strong and confident. I had been training every single day for six months now, acclimatized to the tough conditions, and my stamina was better than ever before. I even think it was better than Wada Sensei's, but my technique had still along way to go, and was not as good. But as Sosai always said: power, stamina, and heart are the most important attributes in a fight.

Sosai knew that Wada was my inspiration, the reason for me being there. I wonder why he matched us up? I can only speculate, but Sosai loved to throw down the challenge and to say, "Anything is possible if you want it bad enough," so I guess he was going to put this to the test. It certainly was one of the most surreal experiences of my life. This was my moment of truth.

When Goda Shihan called our names out, to say we were to fight each other, I have to admit I was OK with this. But this was a serious day – a test – and I had to perform. I blocked it out that my opponent was Wada, and thought of him as just someone I had to defeat at all costs. I wonder what Wada's thoughts were? To this day, I still wonder what was going through his head.

I felt a buzz of nerves course through my body as we lined up, even more so than usual before a big fight. All of the other *uchi deshi*, instructors, and bystanders kneeled in formation at the back of the dojo.

We went hard at each other from the start. I was focused

and determined. Wada's blows did not hurt me, but I was very wary of his dangerous head kicks. We were picking our shots and making them count. As usual, the other *uchi deshi* and those watching remained silent at first, so the sound of our blows ripping into each other as we exhaled hard was the only sound in the dojo. But as the fight went on, the others started yellowing out *"kai"* to inspire and encourage us, or when we landed powerful shots. I was very fit, and I knew how long this round was going to go. Stamina would be a deciding factor. I did not take a backward step, and was the aggressor as much as I could be.

We were pretty even for most of the match, but I then stepped it up in the last minute, pushing Wada back with thunderous punches that barraged his chest and abdomen, and leg kicks that I knew rattled his thighs to the bone. He tried not to show it, but I could see my punches and kicks taking their toll. By the end, I was clearly the dominant fighter, and sure enough, the judges awarded the fight to me. I was selected to fight in the All Japan and Wada wasn't. Wada Sensei graciously congratulated me, but I hope he didn't feel too bad, because he was still everything to me.

I remember the current World Champion, Matsui Senpai, coming up to me later on after that fight and asking how old I was. I replied that I was 19. He seemed surprised, and gave me that look and nod that means "well done." Looking back, that was a pretty amazing time, a real life story where the student finally overcomes the teacher's own ability, through the teacher's own efforts and training. It is something I am extremely humbled by, and will never forget.

CHAPTER 25
THE SADDEST TIME

若獅子

When I first arrived in Japan as an *uchi deshi*, I regularly sent and received letters from my family and friends back home. There were many to and from my mum, of course, and to the first love of my life, Tiffany, and many from my old mates at the Elwood dojo. There was only one phone in the *Honbu*, and overseas calls were very expensive in those days, and since first-year *uchi deshi* couldn't even leave the dojo, there was no point in anyone coming to visit me.

Around October during my first year, about six months in, I would often get letters from home and from my girlfriend, Tiffany. My friend Anton Vojic from the dojo was a crazed Collingwood supporter (a Melbourne Australian rules football team) and I remember getting letters from him as well, nice guy that he was. These days everyone uses cell phones and email, but in those days 'everyone sent handwritten letters. I cherished those letters, and often read them over and over until I fell asleep at night.

One day Kato opened the sliding door of the dorm and said there was a phone call for me. I was surprised, because I hardly every got phone calls, so I got up quickly and went to the phone. It was my friend Trifon.

"Judd, I have some bad news, mate. Anton killed himself last night." I could hear the words he was saying, but my brain couldn't register the meaning – that my good mate Anton from the dojo in Australia had committed suicide. He had shot himself. I was devastated to hear this over the phone.

I ran back toward the dormitory, broke down just around the corner, and bawled my eyes out. I was completely

THE YOUNG LIONS

devastated. I slowly shuffled my feet back to the dorm, even though you were suppose to run and never walk between the *Honbu* and dorm. It was the hardest thing I had ever dealt with. As I entered the dorm I wiped away my tears and tried to act normal. I had no one to console me.

I didn't sleep much that night, trying to cry silently so none of the other *uchi deshi* would hear me. I was still shattered in the morning, feeling hollow.

To make things worse, I had a run-in with the only other Australian in the *Honbu* dojo at that time, a sensei from back home that was visiting for a couple months. He had known Anton Vojic, too. He came up to me before class and said, "I heard Anton killed himself. That's a bummer," then shrugged and walked off nonchalantly.

His statement crippled me even more, making my knees buckle. The only person there who had known Anton, someone whom I had expected to be compassionate, the only person I could even talk to about it, and all he had to say was, "That's a bummer"? A bummer?! The heartless bastard! My knees buckled at the insult to my departed mate, but then I got mad. I felt an uncontrollable fire fill my body, my eyes burning into his back as he walked off. To this day, I don't know what I would have done to him if he hadn't walked away.

Knowing I couldn't return to Australia for Anton's funeral made it almost unbearable. I kept looking at the photo I'd taken of us at the airport, alongside Nick Zav, Trifon, Manny, and Anton, who looked so healthy and alive.

I was just in a state of disbelief, and had no one to talk with about this. I told no one, and this was one of my lowest moments, especially as an *uchi deshi* who had virtually no outside support. I didn't dare tell anyone in the dorm, so I felt completely alone like never before.

My mum actually gave a speech at the funeral on my behalf, which I very much appreciated. I felt completely helpless, and could only mourn silently for my friend Anton, who was so young and had his whole life in front of him. I wished I could turn back the clock and talk to him before he met his tragic demise. Before coming to Japan, I used to often stay over at his house. We would watch *Star Wars* and *The Empire Strikes Back* – his favorite movies – back to back, every time.

We were top mates, and I think about him a lot. It was one of the hardest points in my life and my training as an *uchi deshi*, and the pain of missing my friend wore heavy on me. Although I never wavered through any of the physical or mental training during my 1,000 days that was the closest I came to quitting and going home. As a 19-year-old all on his own, it was really hard to deal with. But I knew that Anton would want me to keep going; he would tell me to keep fighting. Later on, when I fought in tournaments as an *uchi deshi*, I would think of Anton, and know that I was fighting for both of us. This was a very sad time in my first year, but I soldiered on in memory of Anton.

I miss you, my friend.

若獅子

15-year old Judd training with Senpai Trevor in the Elwood squash courts in Australia.

THE YOUNG LIONS

Judd at 15 years old in 1986, playing golf.

Completion of the 100-man kumite in Osaka, Japan (above).

Judd and Nicolas in the Honbu dojo in 1991 (below).

Fight no. 52 of the 100-man kumite (above).

17-year old Judd's quest for Japan (below).

STRATHMORE teenager Judd Reid has his sights set on studying karate in Japan.
Photo: KEITH BROWN

Judd's set to enter school of hard knocks

Wada Sensei in front, Manny in the red top, Gary Flingnar, and a 16-year old Judd in Australia (above).

Sosai Mas Oyama with Sean Connery in the late 1960's in the Honbu dojo (below).

THE YOUNG LIONS

1991 in the dormitory (above) singing the Wakajishi (Young Lion's song). Karuda on the right. Far left side, Mohamad, Judd, Nick and Hashimoto Senpai at the front.

Sandor Brezovai standing at the front of the dormitory. Wakajishiryo written on the front door in Japanese writing (below).

At the summer camp (above). From the left, Sandor, Judd, Ligo and Yui Senpai (The Ranger).

Uchi deshi standing at attention at the morning chore (ceremony) with Sosai (below). From the right, Judd, Ligo, Hashimoto Senpai, and Sandor in the second line at far left.

THE YOUNG LIONS

Saturday night feast with Sosai (above). From the end of the table, Sosai at the back, Mohamad, Sandor, Judd, Ligo and Ishida.

Exhausted first-year uchi deshis getting a nap in whenever they can (below). Kato is on the right, Suzuki on the left and Ishida at the back.

JUDD REID

First year uchi deshis at a swim park in Tokyo in 1990 (above). From the right side back, Judd, Sandor and the Japanese senpais. At the front from left, Ligo and Mohamad.

Awarded with our plaques and certificates on graduation day in 1993 (below). From the left, Judd, Yamakage (Pink Panther), Kato, Suzuki, Komukai, Ishida, Karuda and Oshikiri.

THE YOUNG LIONS

Sosai Oyama in his office on the 3rd floor of the Honbu headquarters in Tokyo (above).

The first-year uchi deshi in 1990. From the front left, Ligo, Judd, Sosai Oyama, Sandor, Suzuki. From back left, Yamakage (Pink Panther), Kato, Komukai and Ishida.

Sosai Oyama congratulating Judd on graduation day 1993 (above).

One month before the 100-man kumite in 2011, Judd playing around during training (below).

THE YOUNG LIONS

1990 first year Uchi Deshi (above). Pink Panther on the right singing the Young Lion's song in the dormitory.

Ten more fights to go during the 100-man fight in 2011 (below).

Judd and the Pink Panther at the front of the honbu in 1991 with Sosai's secretaries (above).

On guard in the dormitory in 1991 (below) - baseball bat close for the number one enemy: the cockroaches!

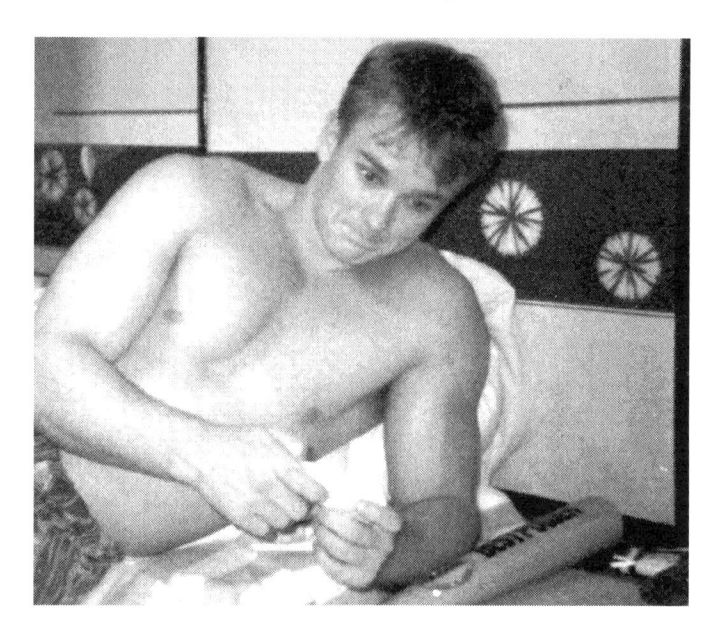

Uchi deshi morning training sessions in the concrete park and at the front of the Honbu in 1990.

Sosai Oyama sitting at the front of the dojo (above).

After Judd completed the 100-man kumite, the Japanese fighters celebrated by throwing him up in the air (below).

Judd's mum with his son, Max.

Judd's wife, Mo, giving him a loving kiss after he finished the 100-Man kumite.

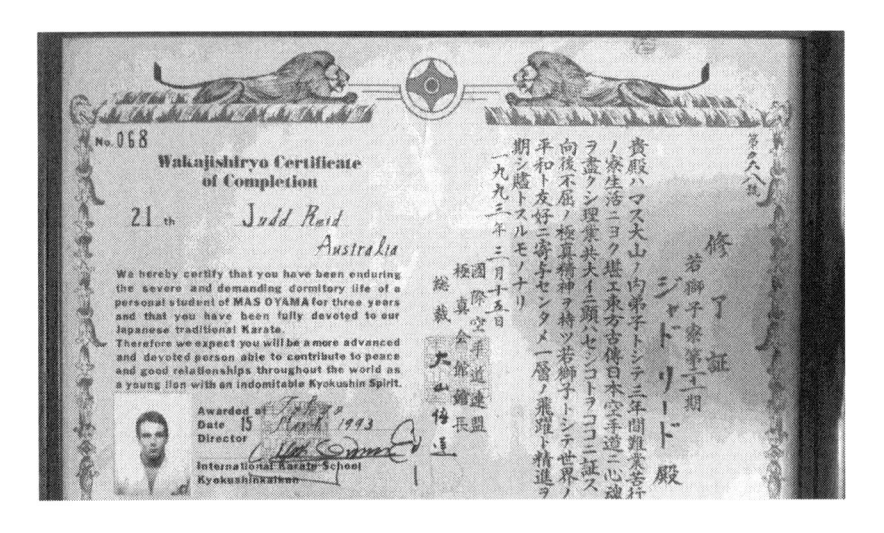

My graduation certificate from Sosai Oyama's Young Lions program (above).

Even at 16-years old, I wrote my hopes and dreams in my diary on the long train rides back home from training each night (below).

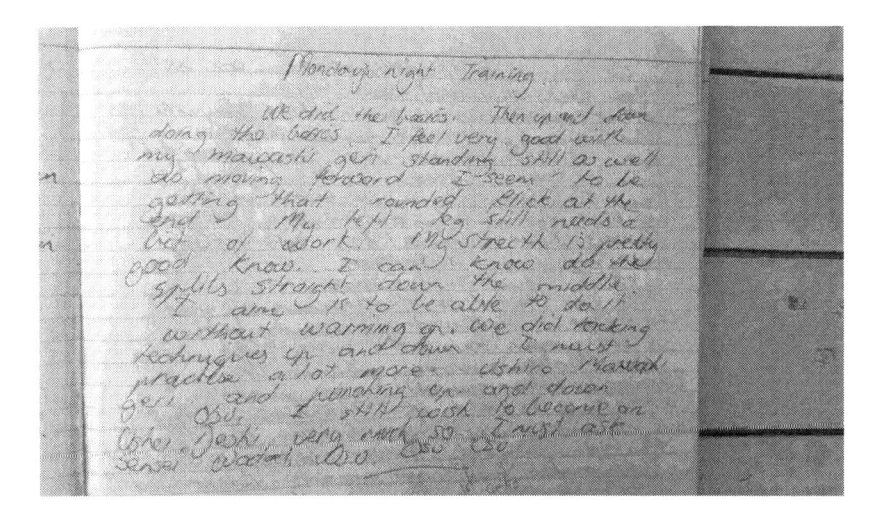

CHAPTER 26
100-MAN KUMITE,
FIGHTS 30 THROUGH 50

若獅子

By fight 30 I was totally in control. Some fights were harder than others, but nothing was hurting me.

My eye was totally in, I wasn't a bit tired, and I was focused and wanted to win every fight. I could see my opponents' facial expressions and hear the groaning noises of pain from some of them when I really connected. This fueled me even more. It just solidified in my mind that I was as strong as I believed and would get through this.

I had fought over 40 guys now, and everything was going according to plan. A few guys tried to take my head off, but that was easiest for me to defend against. I would instantly counter with an inside leg kick, taking out their weight-bearing leg, sending them crashing to the ground.

I was fighting smart and making every technique that I threw count. There were no half measures, and that's why my leg sweeps were so effective. I must have swept 30 of the first 50 fighters off their feet, sending them crumbling to the mat – some more than once. Using technique – not just sheer force – was an important part of my strategy, and it was working beautifully.

After fight number 50 I went to my corner and had a short break. I was allowed five minutes. I didn't sit down. I had a small drink and energy bar and listened to my support team's advice. They said, "You're fighting magnificently, Judd. Keep doing what you're doing." I was very happy to hear this because I felt great, and everything was going according to plan. Nick, Anton, Ned and Paul all gave me the nod of "keep it up, Judd." My mate Anton said, "It looks like you're going to do this easy."

But, unbeknownst to me, what lay ahead was my worst nightmare. To get through the 100 fights, I'd have to endure more pain than I'd ever experienced in my life. It's unimaginable to me now, and it still makes me wince just thinking about it.

CHAPTER 27
THE ALL JAPAN OPEN WEIGHT TOURNAMENT

若獅子

In November 1990, only six months into my training, I had been chosen to fight in the 22nd All Japan Open Weight Tournament. I was perhaps the youngest fighter there, and only a first-year *uchi deshi*. No one had ever heard of this happening before. I'd like to say I did very well, but tournaments in Japan are of a much higher level than anywhere else, and this was Japan's biggest and best.

The Tokyo Metropolitan Gymnasium is a massive world-class sporting complex, originally built in Sedagaya in Tokyo in 1954 for the World Wrestling Championship. It was also used as the venue for gymnastics at the 1964 Tokyo Summer Olympics, and will be used again in 2020. It is a massive, intimidating complex – the perfect place for Sosai Oyama's largest and most prestigious national karate tournament.

Even though the tournament's reputation was revered, I quickly realized just how big of a deal it was. For the opening ceremonies, all of us fighters came out and lined up on the mats, standing next to our first opponent. There was a full 30-piece orchestra on hand serenading us, the music penetrating through shouts of admiration and encouragement from 20,000 spectators, vibrating through my body.

Sosai addressed all the fighters standing in formation, telling us to fight with all our might, to show the spirit of Kyokushin and make him proud. His words further elevated the resolve of all the competitors, and after that my mindset was that there were only two ways I'd go home: in victory or in death. (I guarantee the Japanese fighters were thinking the same!)

In the All Japan there are 128 competitors, the best hand-picked fighters from all over the country including both Japanese and foreigners living in Japan. To win the whole tournament means winning seven fights over two days, a physically near-impossible task. There are two fights in the first day, and potentially five in the second. I won my first fight on decision, convincingly, in the first round, and was thinking very positively. The second fight was against a very experienced fighter weighing in at 175 pounds (80 kg). Remember that the tournaments in those days were open weight class, so at 155 pounds (70 kg) I would have to move around and pick my shots to have any chance. In the end I lost my second fight on decision after one extension. I remember that if I'd won that fight, I would have fought Yamaki Kenji in my next fight – someone who had already won the All Japan, and who went on to become World Champion in 1995.

I'd tried my best and won my first fight, but narrowly lost my second. Perhaps Sosai Oyama wanted to test me and see how I would stand up against Japan's best fighters, and although I had great technique, my opposing fighter in the second round was too strong and experienced for my still-skinny frame.

I couldn't help but feel like I'd let Sosai down. He'd put his trust in me, and I disappointed him. "I should have thrown more combinations, I should have used my kicks better," I thought to myself. "I should have. I should have. I should have!"

But I reminded myself that fighting in this All Japan, walking out onto the big mat together in front of Sosai Oyama and a crowd of 20,000 people, was an overwhelming experience. Sosai encouraged the fighters to give their best and show spirit and do what they could to get into the next year's world tournament. It was an electric, exciting event that I still remember as if it were just yesterday.

The eventual winner was Masuda Akira, with future World

Champion Midori Kenji in second place, and another future World Champion, Yamaki Kenji, also placing highly. Interestingly, Masuda and Yamaki both went on to also complete the 100-man *kumite*. I remember thinking, "This is just my first year in Japan, and I am already fighting with legends." I was hooked on the adrenaline and thrill of it, and ready for more.

CHAPTER 28
THE JAPANESE WAY

若獅子

To really understand the Japanese mentality, you have to spend years living there and be able to speak the language. Their thinking and mindset is so different from a westerner on so many levels. In a lot of ways, Japan may as well be another planet.

The most common and widely known difference is that the Japanese always put the good of the group above the needs of the individual. To understand why, consider this: Japan has a population of about 130 million people living on an island smaller than the Australian state of Victoria or the American state of California. That is a very densely packed population, surviving and striving in cramped conditions that are unimaginable to most of us. There are rules in place, and the rules are followed to keep society in order. If everyone just did what they wanted, like in the west, there would be total anarchy.

The Japanese are taught to be very rigid and formulated from early childhood. They have certain ways of thinking, and a great sense of duty and honor. This indoctrination of rules starts at the beginning of junior high school, and is part and parcel of the Japanese psyche. Elementary school kids in Japan are hyperactive and fun loving, just like those in the west, but that all changes the year they enter junior high. If you watch a Japanese kid from the age of 10 to 12, you will notice a massive change in personality – and that stays with them for life. It is the first year of junior high when they fully realize what life in Japanese culture will be like, and what the world expects of them.

Junior high kids are put under a lot of pressure, and learning is done by rote, which involves memorizing a huge amount of facts and figures, as well as learning all the rules of Japanese society – from school to work, family and social situations. This is not to say that the Japanese educational system pumps out only robots; some of the most artistic and free-thinking people I have met in my life are Japanese, but they are the minority. As an example, if a kid stays on the path of education, and goes to cram school (after-school school) every day, he may just make it into one of the better universities and lead a successful, rich life. However, if he falls off anywhere along the way, there is *no* second chance. I used to look at the millions of Japanese "salarymen" (the term for common business workers) going to work each day on the subway and wonder how they did it. Duty and honor is the answer. The salaryman is the modern-day samurai, and they refuse to ever give up.

To give you a just one simple example of the Japanese system, employees of McDonald's in Japan are given a training manual that runs to more than 700 pages, and they must memorize every possible situation that is listed in the manual in order to work at the front, serving customers. The manual covers every possible situation imaginable, and the correct response to each situation. God help the poor guy at the counter who gets a foreigner that comes in and requests something not covered in the manual!

Salarymen are under extreme pressure, especially as juniors. They must be first into the office each day, last out of the office, and if the boss decides to go out drinking 'til 3 AM, they must accompany him and drink every time their boss does. The junior salaryman may not get home until 3:30 AM, but he must still be back in the office at 7 AM the next day, while the boss can come in at midday if he likes. This is the Japanese work hierarchy in its simplest form.

Rules are prevalent everywhere in Japanese society, and as a foreigner you stay outside of the system only until you have

The Japanese Way

lived there for years and become fluent in the language. But even then you are always a *gaijin,* or outsider – not a bad thing to be, to be honest. Being called a *gaijin* is not an insult, as many foreigners seem to think. It literally means "outside person," and defines you as someone who has not grown up inside the Japanese system, so it means you will be treated a little differently, and often given some leeway.

The *uchi deshi* are an extreme version of this mindset. Their minds are locked like vises, they are trained to show no emotion, and they give nothing away. But they are still human, and they are honor and duty bound. They are there because they are driven, they worship Sosai Oyama, and they want to follow in his footsteps. I've always thought that the Japanese have the ultimate poker face, never showing any emotion, and hence they make such great fighters. It is also an extension of the Japanese *honne* and *tatemae* – one's true feelings vs. those displayed in public, which are complete polar opposites in Japan.

They say that the Japanese order of priorities in life goes from company to country to family to God, ranking from the top down. This may have changed in recent years, but ask any westerner and I'm sure he would say his order was" family first, then country, followed by God". In Japan, *giri,* or duty, always takes precedence over *ninjo,* or emotion. This must really be hard for the Japanese. They will die for a cause, if need be, for the sake of duty and honor rather than live a life chasing their personal desires and emotions. Again, this is said to have changed since my time there in the early 1990s, when the Japanese economy was looking to overtake America and become the biggest in the world, and jobs in Japanese companies were for life.

Of course these rules and ways of society existed in the dojo, too. If an *uchi deshi* was slacking off in class, he'd be ordered to go outside to the park and do jumping squats until told to stop. Sometimes punishment was to do jumping squats in the park at night, for hours on end – literally hours, and sometimes even all night. Punishments also included handstands in the smaller ground floor dojo, where you would be forced to stand on your hands until you collapsed, and then ordered to get up and do it again and again and again. You might also be told to do pushups in the dormitory, which might go into the hundreds while your superiors screamed abused at you in Japanese.

I remember one day Hashimoto Senpai, a second-year uchi deshi, barged into our dorm room in the middle of the night and woke us all up. He started scolding the Pink Panther and Kato for something they had done wrong while on guard duty earlier that day. Hashimoto was absolutely furious and wouldn't calm down, even though the Pink Panther and Kato kept genuflecting and apologizing in the most formal way, with "osu shitsureishimashita "("I'm sorry") over and over. Hashimoto wouldn't hear it, and demanded they start doing pushups. The rest of us in the room were silent as they started cranking out their punishment. After they did about 100 pushups, you could see they were starting to tire. We were all already exhausted from a long day of training, but Hashimoto wanted them to feel pain. Sweat started dripping from their foreheads onto the tatami mats. Their arms were shaking violently, but still they kept on. Not satisfied, Hashimoto kicked Kato in the arm with his boot, saying "Bakairo" (you fool), keep going!"

They couldn't do any more pushups, but their senior tormentor wasn't satisfied – he wanted blood. Hashimoto kept screaming for them to keep going.

They didn't dare disobey and quit, so the Pink Panther and Kato screamed with anguish, pushing themselves to get their chests off the floor again and again. Their bodies gave up long before their will did, and when they both collapsed, it was head first into the tatami mat.

But Hashimoto screamed at them to keep going. So they rested only for a couple seconds, and then squeezed out a few more pushups before collapsing again, and resting for a breath before going on. I'd completely lost count of how many

The Japanese Way

pushups they'd done now. I wanted to help them, but what could I do?

Finally, Hashimoto stormed out of the room. Incredibly, the Pink Panther and Kato stayed in pushup position, straining and screaming in pain as they fought to stay off the floor. I couldn't believe my eyes, but they 'couldn't stop because Hashimoto had never specifically given that order.

After about 30 seconds, Hashimoto came back into the dorm. When he saw them there, fighting to stay in a plank position, he told them to stop and then walked out again.

My two uchi deshi classmates collapsed for the final time, and slowly rolled onto their backs, their faces masks of pain and covered in sweat. There was complete silence in the room.

Instructions like these never came directly from Sosai Oyama, but from the system of Japanese hierarchy, which was magnified in the setting of the *uchi deshi*. I'm sure Sosai knew about it, but I doubt he ever gave direct instructions for such punishments. This is just the Japanese way. To be an *uchi deshi*, you needed to accept this. Rules are ingrained into Japanese life and they are there for a good reason. If you weren't prepared to accept this, you wouldn't last long as a Young Lion.

First-year *uchi deshi* were like machines; they were slaves, and obedient to their seniors. But it was not a dynamic that was frowned upon in Japan. If you have ever visited that country and seen the Japanese service workers, you will get an inkling of how this works. If you enter a Lawson store there (which is like a 7-Eleven or convenience store), all the staff will yell out and greet you with *irashaimasen*, which means, "welcome to our store." The staff will then literally run around trying to serve you as quickly and politely as possible. I've always said, whether it's a five-star hotel or a local shop down the road, in Tokyo the service will be the same.

So keeping this in mind, first-year *uchi deshi* were expected to be like worker bees: obedient, never missing a step, and on the lookout for their seniors at all times, like a tiger waiting to pounce. Karate dojos around the world have a lot of Japanese etiquette like this, but this was another level altogether. Everything had to be done with speed and precision, just like training. As I have said, in the dorm, eating was done at a fast pace so we didn't linger and could attend to our seniors. Showering had to be done quickly, so as not to cause any inconvenience – in case a senior might be waiting. Even going to the toilet was get in and get out! There was no down time, except when you slept. It was full on!

I have to admit, the Japanese had a harder time than us westerners in the first year, because of their upbringing. They were given more errands and tasks because they could speak Japanese and knew their way around, and I think we foreigners were much more open and adaptable because everything was completely new and different. However, since I was there in my formative years, a lot of what I experienced stuck with me for life. To this day, I still carry some of these Japanese traits, and I like them. There is a lot of tradition and respect involved, and I think it's important not to lose this.

Sosai Oyama always said that karate starts with respect towards each other, and then ends with respect – hence the bowing at the start and finish of class, shaking each other's hands with two hands, a bow, and saying *domo arigato gozaimashita* to each other, which means "thank you very much." Sosai used to say that if everyone did karate, there would be no wars. Everyone could just duke it out in the dojo instead. "Perfect," I thought. "The whole world should be like this, and there would be no wars!"

I think the spirit and philosophies of Kyokushin are best expressed by two very short, but powerful, words we use: *osu* and *kiai*. People always ask me what these two Japanese karate verbalizations mean. But I think that until they have seen a karate tournament or a karate class, they'll never truly understand.

Osu is a Japanese word in its most unique and polite form. The word *hai* means "yes" in the Japanese language, and is used most commonly. But in the martial arts world, we have replaced *hai* with *osu*. *Osu* can mean many things: to persevere, not give up, endure or overcome. It can also mean, "yes, I understand"; "yes, I can do it" "sorry, I don't understand" or "yes, I will try." It's basically an acknowledgement, and its meaning depends on the tone of voice in which you use it.

For example, if I'm teaching and I'm talking to the students who are about to go out and fight, giving them encouraging words and trying to pump them up, the student will acknowledge me and yell out *osu*, maybe even repeating the word a few times. It's powerful word, which gives you belief in yourself, and you will carry that out onto the mat with you, and into any challenge you might come across. It reflects, once again, that phrase we use often: Never give up!

Kiai is similar, but is used in different circumstances. *Kiai* is yelled out in class when practicing techniques. I always tell the new students who start training not to hold onto their breath when doing punching or kicking drills, but to yell *kiai* instead. I tell the new students not to be shy, and to yell the word out loud, concentrating on getting their power from the bottom of their abdominals, mustering all their energy. Soon enough they realize that yelling this word, *kiai,* gives them power and focus. I myself have been in exhausting situations, and have found that screaming out *kiai* or *ishaa* (a similar word) has lifted my spirits and has given me that edge that I needed when I felt I was almost done.

I've seen in kids' tournaments, little ones as young as six years old giving it their best, but looking tired and almost like they're about to give up. The teacher will order the kid to yell out *kiai, kiai!* The kid hears this and starts to *kiai,* and suddenly their spirits lift. Tears might even be running down their face, not due to pain but more their adrenaline, emotions, and their being overwhelmed by the whole experience of fighting. But I tell you what, yelling the word *kiai* gets them across the line. They stand strong and proud at the end of the fight, spectators are amazed and overwhelmed with these kids' fighting spirit, and of course the parents are super proud of their children.

Sometimes I even see parents in tears, too. Hence these symbolic and powerful words, *osu* and *kiai*. Persevere and never give up! *Osu!*

CHAPTER 29
MOVING UP THE RANKS
AS A YOUNG LION

若獅子

"I realized that perseverance and step-by-step progress are the only ways to reach a goal along a chosen path." –Sosai Oyama

In the Young Lions, each year was markedly different. The first year we were slaves; we were nothing. You had to do what your seniors said, and couldn't even go to the shops to buy a soft drink or a chocolate bar. I wasn't allowed to stand at the front of the *Honbu* and socialize or chitchat.

But as a second-year student I could go to the shops and walk around the neighborhood with no supervision needed. As a third-year I could stand at the front of the *Honbu* and talk to anyone I wanted, but if a senior was around – especially a former *uchi deshi* – I still had to be on my toes. But this was still more at ease, compared to the first-years, who were looking out for everyone. I remember walking casually back and forth from the dorm to the dojo, when I would hear a clatter behind me and a first-year would run by me, yelling *shitsureishimasu* as he passed (the most polite form of "'excuse me'" in Japanese). What a different world I lived in! It felt like forever while I was there, and a lifetime ago now.

It wasn't always dead serious all the time, though. There were many moments of hilarity and light-heartedness, especially if there were no seniors around to attend to. I remember one day, about six months into my first year, I was at the top of the dorm about 9 PM, just falling asleep, when I was awakened by these loud screams and yelling from in my room,

THE YOUNG LIONS

only a few feet away from me. I was wondering what the hell was going on, if there was a fire or we were being attacked or something. I could hear people yelling and running around, and finally, one of the *uchi deshi* flicked on the light. They were frantically darting around, with pure panic on their faces. I yelled, "What's wrong? What's wrong?" They replied, "*Kokiburi, kokiburi,*" meaning "cockroach, cockroach." I stood there dumbfounded for a second, thinking "What? Cockroach? What do they mean? Are these superhuman, tough *uchi deshi* actually scared of cockroaches?" They stood back while I picked up the nearest and deadliest weapon I could find – a karate magazine – hunted down my ferocious prey, and smashed it into smithereens, saving all of our lives and becoming a hero for all time. I still look back and laugh, that these guys who could fight just about anyone, anywhere, anytime, were actually scared of a bug.

A few days later, we were all given small, foot-long baseball bats, with the instructions that it would come in handy should we ever have an intruder enter the dorm. But I knew this was not for intruders; it was to keep those vicious cockroaches, the ultimate enemy of the Japanese *uchi deshi,* at bay!

I started in The Young Lions course when I had just turned 19 years old. Most of the other first-years were the same age, except Suzuki and Kumokai, who were about 22 – which seemed old to me at the time, but really they were just kids, too. I think Sosai Oyama wanted the *uchi deshi* to start young because at that age you are hungry and eager and willing to take on all challenges. There are no "what ifs," no "buts," and no hesitation. You are fearless and naïve, and that in this case it's a good thing, because you will take on any challenge or obstacle with no questions asked. You'll just say *osu* and do it. Not only that, but you can be molded, and that's what Sosai wanted. The older you get, the more you weigh up the consequences of your actions. Doubts creep into your mind, and you have other responsibilities you need to take care of. At 18 or 19 years old, you're a young foot soldier, ready and willing to take any challenge thrown your way.

Sosai Oyama sure had a plan: he was going to create his own army of well-trained and disciplined karate commandos who would carry on the traditions and spread the martial arts that he had created, that he had poured his whole heart and soul into. Who better to do this than his private students, who had sacrificed three years of their life? One of Sosai Oyama's famous sayings was, "One becomes a beginner after one thousand days of training, and an expert after ten thousand days of practice." Sosai could count on us Young Lions, who became beginners after our first thousand days, and we would do our utmost to carry on his legacy and do him proud for the rest of our lives.

CHAPTER 30
SECOND-YEAR PROMOTION AND ARRIVAL OF AN ALLY

若獅子

The Japanese New Year, as in the west, is celebrated on January 1st. But in Japan, most people visit a shrine from December 31st to January 3rd to pray for a lucky and a fruitful year ahead. However, for schools, universities, and companies, the New Year begins on April 1st. This just happens to be when the Japanese *sakura,* or cherry blossom trees, are in full bloom. The whole of Tokyo lights up in beautiful bright pink at this time and everybody has a smile on their face.

The cherry blossoms have great significance to the Japanese. People get very excited about the first blossoms, as they signify the end of winter and the beginning of a new year. The Japanese go as far as to say that the cherry blossoms are a metaphor for life. They say that, like the cherry blossoms, life is very beautiful – but very short.

For me the New Year meant my graduation from being a first-year *uchi deshi*, and honestly, the emotion I felt most was relief. Just the fact that I could leave the *Honbu* to buy a chocolate bar without permission seemed like an incredible privilege. I had graduated from a first-year foot soldier to a second-year *uchi deshi* with seniority, privileges, and nine new first-year *uchi deshi* under me to do all the dirty jobs I did in my first year. It didn't mean I was king of the hill just yet; I still had my third-year seniors and *Honbu* teachers above me, but I was given a few more freedoms, could leave the *Honbu* for short periods between classes, and could even take a half-day off every two weeks. Most importantly, this meant no more staring at the clock with the Pink Panther in that godforsaken basement.

But the best part of entering my second year was the arrival of Nicholas Pettas from Denmark. When Nicholas left Denmark he was a brown belt, so he was only one step beneath black belt. But he was far ahead of the other nine *uchi deshi* in his year, already a gifted *karateka* from a Kyokushin Karate background, with some of the highest kicks I had ever seen.

Nick had a Greek father who had died when he was a baby. It was a fact that many of the *uchi deshi* lacked father figures as kids, though I don't know if that was a coincidence or something that drove us to karate and training so hard. Nick and I got along famously, straight from day one. He had a great sense of humor, with a lot of engaging stories from his childhood, and I took him under my wing and taught him the ways of the first-year *uchi deshi*. Nick had a thing for rap music and loved Ice-T and all those other rappers. So, for fun, we learned the lyrics to some Ice-T songs. I didn't mind the 90's rap music, but still to this day I can rap off some Ice-T songs!

Since I was now a second-year, Nick could leave the dojo in my company, and we used to wander around our Ikebukuro suburb just to escape the dormitory and monotony of *uchi deshi* life. In the dorm itself, we both had the same passion for karate, and although he was my rival in some ways, Nick and I were also great mates and pushed each other incredibly hard, doing well in tournaments later on, and doing the *uchi deshi* very proud.

Nick and I fought each other very hard in the dojo, and although I had it over him in his first year, by his second year we were some of the strongest in the dojo, and could stand toe to toe with just about anyone there.

Nick arrived at 155 pounds (70 kg) and immediately dropped to 148 pounds (67 kg), just like I'd dropped 10 pounds in my first months. But by the end of the three years, I graduated at 195 pounds (88k kg) and Nick at 220 pounds (100 kg). Nick and I are asked, to this day, "How did you do it?" and I always tell people, "You have no idea how much food we actually consumed." We ate huge amounts of rice, bowl after bowl, and while the cuisine may not have been five-star, it sure did fill us up and give us fuel for workouts.

In the first year I didn't do any weight training, but by the second and third year we trained weights in the basement. There was an old bench press, a squat rack, dip bars, chin up bar, and dumbbells. We also had a heavy bag for honing our kicks, and we'd kick these mesh bags filled with sand and small rocks' over and over to condition our shins. Between the weight training in the basement and eating like monsters, we put on a lot of weight without sacrificing any speed or stamina.

Even though I was an Aussie and he was European, Nick and I had a lot in common. We both grew up without fathers (Nick's dad had died when he was three), and I guess that really shaped our attitudes and drive early on. More than that, though, we both were easy to get along with, with a similar goofy sense of humor; we bounced things off each other; we both understood the Japanese system perfectly; and – probably most importantly – we were soon were the only two foreign *uchi deshi* in the *Honbu*, making us a target for some of the Japanese. So we really stuck together, knowing that everyone else was gunning for us, and sometimes we told each other before class, "Let's fight hard and let them know who's boss!"

Nick and I were young, with fire in our bellies and chips on our shoulders, and this was exactly the same with the Japanese *uchi deshi*. We were there for a purpose, and that purpose was to become the toughest, strongest and best fighters in the world. There were a lot of hardships, but without pushing ourselves past our limits which instilled the confidence to go head to head with any Japanese or foreign fighter, we couldn't have achieved what we did.

There was no resting; as weeks and months progressed, we set the bar higher and higher. That became our normal, our only aim. There was no point in training and stagnating. Like Oyama said, you either keep going forward, or you slip backwards. The goal was always to become the best in the world, without exception. We didn't train for anything less. Looking back, there were times when we may have been a bit excessive, sending some of the *soto deshi*, or "outside students," back home with a few more bruises than they could handle. But that's what Sosai Oyama was instructing us to do, and we wanted him to be proud. Nick actually wrote a book about our experiences, and says in it that The Razorback often smashed people, and perhaps we were a little bully-like in our actions. But just as others treated us that way at first, we soon dished out most of the punishment as we progressed into seniors. That's just the way it was.

Of course we never were cruel or picked on any lower belts with anything but good intentions, and usually showed great respect and solidarity with out fellow *uchi deshi*. But in a few cases, outsiders came in and really tried their best to take advantage of the younger *uchi deshi*. I guess they were trying to prove that they were better than Sosai Oyama's own students, but little did they know that they had the other *uchi deshi* in the class watching. So when it came their turn to fight Nick, the Pink Panther, The Razorback or me, we would unleash exactly what they had dished out earlier to the juniors – and more. It was like a big brother who roughs up his little brother, but when someone else tries to bully him, the big brother defends him ferociously. Despite the separations by year, all of us *uchi deshi* were in this together. We may have been from a number of different cultures and backgrounds, but we were all like brothers.

In the dormitory we were always living on top of each other, and there may have been times when we got under each other's skin, but we were truly brothers. Even later in life, when we all went on to different careers and countries, we'll always have that unbreakable bond. We are, and always will be, the Young Lions of Sosai Mas Oyama.

CHAPTER 31
ELVIS, ANIME AND SALARYMEN; WELCOME TO TOKYO

若獅子

It was a wild time in Tokyo. Japan is a unique country to begin with, including a society that values tradition and obedience for the greater good more than any other philosophy. In fact, for thousands of years, the island nation of Japan shunned foreigners, even as China and southeast Asian countries welcomed (or were colonized by) the French, English, German, and Dutch. But the Japanese were never conquered throughout their history, thanks in part to the warrior class of samurai charged to protect the society with their lives. The Japanese even thought themselves superior to the more "barbaric" westerners, and considered their emperor a god as well as a leader.

Throughout the centuries Japan thrived, making incredible advances in technology, industry, art and agriculture. Even when I was there in the early 1990s, there were virtually no poor people and no homeless in Japan, and as I mentioned, civil disobedience like graffiti, robbery, and petty crime were unheard of. Women could walk alone on the streets at any time of night without a single worry, there was no violent crime among average citizens, and any drugs that might exist were hidden deep underground.

But in contrast to the placid and traditional Japanese society, life in Tokyo with its 31 million residents was equal parts fascinating, bizarre, energizing and entertaining. For a foreigner like myself, Tokyo's mix of old and new, and extremes in work, food, art, fashion, and technology created a dizzying circus-like atmosphere on her streets.

THE YOUNG LIONS

My first year, it was a special treat just to get a chance to leave the dojo for anything other than training, and walking down the street, I tried not to miss a single detail of the kaleidoscope of culture. Oppressed by conformity to a fault, the Japanese really go over the top when they do let their hair down.

My favorite neighborhoods were Harajuku (a train ride away) and Shinjuko, which sat an easy walk from the dojo. They were like the Times Square or King's Cross of Tokyo, with every new trend, craze, mania or fetish you could imagine on display.

I remember while I was there, Japanese teens and young women were dressing like Alice in Wonderland, with huge tent-like lace dresses and white powdered faces with stark red lipstick. There were also the "Shinjuko Girls," as they were called for their avant-garde fashion sense, dressing like aliens with towering platform shoes. In fact, so many young Japanese women were wearing these shoes that emergency rooms started filling up with girls who had taken tumbles as they tried to walk, breaking their ankles. I think it may have been more dangerous being a Shinjuko Girl than an *uchi deshi!*

Strolling down the street to hit my favorite noodle shop or buy a chocolate bar at the local convenience store, I might pass three Elvis impersonators done up in full garb, complete with pompadour haircuts and blue suede shoes, as the Japanese are maniacal Elvis fans.

Others dressed like their favorite colorful *anime* characters, or read graphic novels as thick as phonebooks, called *manga*.

Most Japanese women still commonly wore traditional kimonos, once they turned twenty years of age, carrying dainty parasols and taking tiny steps in their wooden high-heeled sandals. Yet there were plenty of women in the working world, too, employed in offices, stores, restaurants, and just about anywhere else. The men wore their dignified traditional male kimonos on special holidays or festivals as well, but dressed for work in sharp black suits on a daily basis.

Tokyo was also insanely expensive in 1990, as the country was enjoying time of unprecedented prosperity based on technology and manufacturing, creating an economic bubble that drove real estate prices in Tokyo to the highest in the world. At the time, a steak meal at a nice restaurant might cost 5,000 yen, or $50, while it probably only cost $15 or less in the U.S. My craving for a simple chocolate bar left me $3 lighter in the wallet, and I remember seeing a single cantaloupe on sale for 7,000 yen ($70 USD), though it was displayed and packaged in a designer box with ribbons like it was a luxury watch, not a simple piece of fruit.

Just about everything you could imagine was sold in the ubiquitous vending machines, from soft drinks and snacks to the latest movie on DVD, clothing of all sizes, hot ramen noodles, and even alcohol – as well as some more risqué items I won't mention.

In fact, even now – 25 years later – Japanese prices are about the same as they were in 1990! They haven't even changed the prices on the vending machines in more than two decades, as a soda is still 200 yen, or $2 USD, just as it was in 1990.

But the thing I remember most is that the Japanese businessmen were absolute worker bees – an army of faceless, nameless black haircuts in black suits shuffling to and from work at ridiculous hours, packed into the shiny and spotless trains. Like a subservient herd that knew not to go near the electric fence, hundreds of thousands of these businessmen would line up in perfect formation on the train platforms of Tokyo every morning and evening, waiting for the trains that arrived with such precisions that you could set your watch to them.

The squadron of Japanese worker drones would only break ranks to pack onto the train, literally jostling and shoving each other to squeeze in, a claustrophobic mass that would never work in the west. But once the train departed, they were literally silent. No one spoke; no one hummed to themself or even coughed. I remember closing my eyes on the train, letting the complete silence of hundreds of people wash over me, but feeling like I was totally alone, transported a world away from the rough clacking and noisy conversations of my daily train rides to the dojo in St. Kilda in Australia.

The Japanese lived and died to serve their companies, working tirelessly for the sake of brining honor and success to their employer. Everything else in their lives came in a distant second, including family, health, and definitely any personal interests or free time. It wasn't uncommon for Japanese to work 80 hours a week, arriving at the office by 6 AM to work tirelessly until official business concluded.

But even after official business hours were over, the workday was far from done for the Japanese businessman, who often had to stay into the night to work at his desk or go out to socialize with his superiors. The Japanese worker was expected to cater to every whim and wish of their bosses, and that often included after-hours drinking sessions. For such a rigid, expressionless society, boozing was a socially acceptable way of blowing off steam. The restaurants, bars, and karaoke joints were filled with businessmen getting wild, swigging beer, whiskey, or sake every single time their boss did. It would be a terrible display of etiquette not to keep up, drink for drink, with the boss or to try to leave early, but getting sloshed was perfectly acceptable.

In fact, Tokyo's train platforms were filled with disheveled and inebriated businessmen late at night – a stark contrast to the early morning scene. Even when they passed out or relieved the contents of their stomachs all over the sidewalk or the train platform, no one blinked an eye or looked down on them with any shame – it was just a necessary party of business, and they understood it was the only relief valve on the pressure cooker life of a Japanese company man.

Somehow, they found their way home in the wee hours of the morning – if at all. But they'd wake after only a few hours sleep, throw on a fresh black suit, get to the train station, and start the workday anew. They did this six days a week, 300 days a year, for 40 years. Their commitment to the task was absolute.

In many respects, I began to recognize that the hierarchy and rules in the dojo mirrored those valued in Japanese society, and it all made a lot more sense to me.

CHAPTER 32
TAKING CLASSES IN THE HONBU

若獅子

A couple of months into my second year, Sosai Oyama wanted me to start teaching classes at the *Honbu*. He said I must be able to say the *dojo kun* (the Kyokushin oath) in Japanese perfectly before I could begin teaching. He told both Nick and I to study it hard, and be able to say it by heart and word-perfect. So we did, and I started taking classes in about June 1991.

Soon, I had the *dojo kun* down pat. I think I even sounded Japanese. OK, maybe I couldn't speak Japanese perfectly, but I could say the *dojo kun* using all the technical terminology in karate, and even explain thoroughly how to execute every technique.

One time when I was teaching the class early in my second year, an *uchi deshi* entered the dojo and interrupted the class, which was rare, saying that Sosai wanted to see me. I told the whole class to kneel down, and I quickly ran upstairs to Sosai's office, which was one floor above the dojo. He would have his inside window open, so he could hear pretty much everything that was going on in the dojo underneath him. Sosai told me to increase the basics to 30 repetitions of each, and not to do 20 anymore. He also said, "You're doing a great job. Make them work hard, Judd." I replied with a big loud *osu* and returned to the dojo to continue the class, encouraged that Sosai appreciated my teaching, and my Japanese.

Sosai would not hesitate to pull you up to his office, even scold you, if you messed up the count at all, or if you weren't giving it your best. He would say *bakayaro*, which means "you idiot," and tell you to do it again. But he would just as often reward you with encouraging words when he was pleased. He would say, "Train hard enough, and one day you will be world champion." I remember feeling very proud once when he said to the whole class, "Train hard, and you will be like Juddo."

They say that practice makes perfect, but that's actually not true at all – or, at least, it's incomplete. In fact, perfect practice makes perfect, and too often in karate, other sports or anything else in life, people drill the wrong form or technique over and over again. That's just a very good way to perfect very bad habits, and it's why Sosai insisted we repeated the fundamentals until our form was perfect. So I would emphasize this a lot in my classes, since there's no use building a tall skyscraper if the foundation is shaky. That's how I liked to teach, because it was a reflection of how Sosai taught and his whole philosophy on karate – to do things with perfect technique, and then practice them over and over.

I didn't feel like an outsider since the dojo and Japanese karate was my whole life, but I wonder what the Japanese thought of me, as an outsider, taking classes? Or other foreigners, who would travel thousands of miles to train in Japan, only to see a young-faced kid from Australia teaching the class at the headquarters of Kyokushin in Japan? I think about it now, and I guess it's kind of amazing, and I feel very honored that Sosai had the belief and trust in me to make me a teacher at the *Honbu* at only 20 years old, while most of the regular teachers that weren't *uchi deshi* were 25 to 60 years old.

I have to say, I was very pleased to see that in the classes I was teaching, the numbers grew. Visiting foreigners would ask to get photos taken with me at the end of class, so I guess they thought it was something special to take a class with me.

Sosai left it up to me to teach whatever I wanted, except for that one time he pulled me up and told me to make sure the basics drills were no less than 30. I look back now, and those really were different days – a very special time. From the age of 15, I had a dream. My only dream was to go to Japan to train under the great Sosai Oyama. Five years later, I was not only an *uchi deshi,* but I was teaching classes at the world headquarters of Kyokushin Karate, too.

CHAPTER 33
100-MAN KUMITE, FIGHTS 51 THROUGH 59

若獅子

At fight 51 I came out and bowed to my opponent, ready to take on my last 50 fighters the same way I had the first 50. At this stage it didn't even bother me that I had 50 hard fights to go, but I realized I had to keep my focus, not drop my guard, and keep doing what I was doing.

I had fought each fighter once now, pretty much dominating each fight, but in the second half they would be looking to step it up and fight me as hard as possible. Since I'd leg swept many of the fighters off their feet in the first 50 fights, I'm sure they were looking out for that tactic, intent not to let me do that again.

I remember taking a few hard high kicks to the head in the mid 50s. They didn't hurt me, but I was a little surprised that my reactions had slowed, though I still managed to take my opponent's bottom leg out.

One fight I remember very clearly. My opponent kicked me fair in the head, but I came back with a quick counter kick, taking his bottom leg out from underneath him and sending him sprawling awkwardly. I noticed that a few people in the audience laughed, and the officials, too. For the first 50 fights, I hadn't heard or noticed anything, and it was like I was alone with my opponent. The center judge awarded him with a *wazari* and me with a *wazari*, both half points, so we were even. The fight was called a draw. It was the first bout that I didn't win outright. That wouldn't affect my quest to complete the 100-man fight, as I only needed to survive, not go 100 to nothing, but I remember thinking that they were really turning up the pressure now.

On the next short break, my corner suggested that I change my *gi* top. I looked down and saw that it was covered in splatters of blood and ripped completely on one side, hanging off me. I hadn't even noticed.

CHAPTER 34
A THORN AMONG ROSES

若獅子

At times I would be teaching a class, yelling out the count and different orders, techniques and such, and I would walk over to the window and look down onto the small street that ran alongside the dojo. There, I could watch people walking by. Since I yelled out instructions in Japanese, sometimes the pedestrians on the street would look up and see me and be surprised it was a foreigner speaking such fluent and traditional Japanese, and I'd give these strangers a nod out of courtesy.

Other times it was the girls from the arts and acting school up the road walking by, and I would have a brief stare – without missing a count in the class. You could say I was multitasking. I was always very professional in the class, but in my head I was thinking, "Wow, she looks all right." I was, after all, a 20-year-old full of hormones, sometimes feeling the world was at my feet and feeling strong. You can't blame me; I'm only human!

As *uchi deshi*, we weren't supposed to have any relationships with girls whatsoever. That's a pretty impossible request, considering that we were all 19- to 20-year-old kids with raging hormones. But still, The Ranger told us in no uncertain terms that we were not allowed to have any girlfriends or even interact with girls. If he caught us, there would be some serious repercussions. That wasn't a temptation I had to resist for my first year, since I wasn't even allowed to leave the dojo – not even to go to the Lawson (a popular convenience store in Japan, similar to 7-Eleven) to get a Snickers or Slurpee. But by the second year I had more freedom, as I could go to the shops without asking for permission. So what do you think a healthy 20-year-old does unsupervised in Tokyo?

Oddly enough, The Ranger wasn't always a bully. He was often kind to us in my first year, sometimes even buying us ice cream, which made his cruel behavior even more puzzling. Every Sunday, all the *uchi deshi* were taken by The Ranger to the local *sento,* or Japanese bath house. It was a very popular tradition among Japanese and, separated by sex, you would spend an hour or two relaxing, soaking and warming up in the winter, along with dozens of other naked Japanese, who would be staring at us *gaijin* curiously the whole time. There was a young girl working at the counter there, about the same age as me, named Satoshi, with beautiful long, black hair and a sweet personality. I could tell she liked me, so after seeing her from week to week, I would get out of the *sento* 10 minutes early and make conversation with her.

She knew what I was doing, and that I had a strict lifestyle, because the *uchi deshi* had been going there for years. After a few weeks, she slipped me her home phone number on a piece of paper. I remember I called her on the public phone, which cost 10 yen in those days (10 cents U.S.) for only a minute, and being dirt poor I always had to keep the conversation short and sweet. Now, in my second year I could have half a day off every two weeks, which I did on a Wednesday from after lunch until dinner. So I used that opportunity to meet Satoshi. We would go and see a movie, followed by some hanky-panky in one of Tokyo's many love hotels that we could rent by the hour.

This private relationship went on until just before graduation, for about a year and a half, and she was a lovely girl. Having some female companionship helped my morale greatly during my tenure. Nick and the Pink Panther knew about my relationship with Satoshi, but to this day no one else has ever known. I don't know where she is today, but I hope she is happy and living a great life.

While I did appreciate Satoshi and we had some good times, it wasn't close to the feelings I'd had for Tiffany, the love of my life up until then. While there wasn't much room for romantic long-distance correspondence as an *uchi deshi*, of course I never forgot about her. In fact, she was often in my thoughts. When I left for Japan in 1990, she kept in contact often, sending me encouraging letters and pictures of herself, and I would reply when I could. These sorts of letters were very important that first year, as it was a very lonely time indeed. She also sent me a little photo album of myself, and I remember showing Mohamad and Ligo the pictures, and her beauty blew them away.

It just so happens that Tiffany reentered my life when she came over to Japan for three months to do some modeling in 1991. We got together once at a coffee shop when I had a half day off. We caught up and soon were talking and laughing like old times, and I ended up at Tiffany's apartment.

We were intimate again, just like the old days, and I remember thinking, "I'll just have a short nap before heading back to the dojo…" Instead I woke in a panic at 3 AM, realizing I was going to be in deep trouble at the *Honbu*. The rules about these half days off were very strict, and I didn't know how I was going to get around this. Tiffany wanted me to stay. I looked at her again, there in the predawn blackness, the glow from Tokyo's neon lights outside tracing her curves.

She wanted me to stay. Hell, I wanted me to stay, too, but I knew what was at stake. Leaving this beautiful and wonderful girl not just once, but twice in a lifetime was more than I could bear. But if I stayed with her in that warm, comfortable bed, I'd be going back on everything I'd pledged to Sosai Oyama and the Young Lions. It was one of the toughest decisions of my life.

I jumped up, said goodbye to Tiffany, and kissed her on the forehead. I told her we'd get together before she left Japan and quickly headed out the door, not daring to look back because I didn't trust myself. I caught the first train at 5 AM back to the *Honbu*. I sat with my head in my hands, thinking. I knew deep down that I wouldn't be able to see Tiffany again. I had given up everything in Oz to be here in Japan and chase my dream, and there was only room for that in my life. A long-distance relationship was never going to work, and wouldn't have been fair to Tiffany. If I was to graduate soon maybe it could be a different story, but I still had 18 months to go. She deserved better.

It was the last time I ever saw her. This time, she didn't even send me letters anymore.

It was still dark when I arrived at the *Honbu,* the cherry blossoms sleeping, and my breath like smoke in the cold. I was late, but thankfully the morning workout in the park hadn't started yet. I snuck up to the clothesline that hung outside our dojo and grabbed my *gi* pants off the line, slipping my civilian pants off and getting into uniform right there on the street. When the rest of the *uchi deshi* soon filed out, I was already stretching, as though I had just woken and got out there early, the most dedicated of Young Lions.

CHAPTER 35
SUMMER AND WINTER CAMPS

若獅子

Every year Sosai held both a summer and winter training camp. The summer camp was held in August, usually at the beach somewhere in Chiba – about three hours from Tokyo. The winter camps were in January, and held somewhere up north with lots of snow. About 150 to 300 students would turn up. It was always about 95% Japanese from dojos around the country, and usually about 10 to 15 foreigners would also be specifically invited by Sosai to travel overseas to attend as well.

Training at the camps often involved runs up to 13 miles, training in the surf in summer, and standing under waterfalls in the winter. More than anything else, these were bonding sessions for Japanese Kyokushin Karate*ka*, and have since been adopted around the world.

In August 1991 the summer camp was a little different, because the World Championship was going to be held in November, and so all the top Japanese fighters from around the country were there. Since the standard of fighter was so high, and they were all training with the aim to be World Champion in a few months, it was the hardest camp that I could ever remember.

We would wake up at ridiculous hours – usually around 3:45 AM – and the whole morning session was done in the dark. We would run down to the beach, and then along the beach perhaps two to three miles in the sand for an initial warm-up. I remember the hardest thing was actually not being able to see, except for nights with a full moon. And, of course, the soft sand didn't help matters. The head instructor who was at the front would yell out "Fighto!" and as we ran we would repeat it after him very loudly. The attendance at this camp was the biggest I can ever remember, at about 300, so you had 300 guys in their karate *gi* running down the beach at 4 AM in the dark yelling "Fighto Fighto Fighto!" Every now and then the leader would yell in a big loud voice, dragging the words out: "Kyokusshiiiiiiin Fighto!" which we, again, would reply to with an even louder almighty "FIGHTO!"

So we would run down the beach and back, and then we would all get into formation facing toward the water. The *Senpai* would always stand in the water, leading the class through the basics punches, blocks, and kicks while we would be on the sand following his instructions. He would then order us into the water to join him, and we would all go down to do push-ups in the water. Even though it was summer, the water in Chiba was cold', so it was absolutely freezing at 4 AM. There are also some pretty decent waves in Chiba, as parts of the coast are renowned surfing areas, so often we would also get buffeted and swamped by waves as we were doing our push-ups and squats.

I remember doing my push-ups and looking at my fellow students beside me, trying to stay in formation and yelling *kiai* as they completed each rep, but as the waves crashed into them they tumbled and spilled into the ocean. It was kind of funny, but the Japanese didn't laugh – just picked themselves up, got back in formation, and continued with the exercise.

Now and then I took a sneak peek at the head instructor, and couldn't help but notice him having a wry chuckle at our expense. I think he wasn't just laughing at the other students, but also the fact that he was deepest in the water and doing the push-ups, so he must have been laughing at his own predicament as well.

But, of course, it was the Japanese way not to show emotion.

We also had to drink with the seniors at these summer camps. Just as etiquette dictates that Japanese businessmen need to drink with their bosses, the first year *uchi deshi* had to match the senior students and instructors swig for swig when they drank, slamming down an alarming number of beers. The

Japanese turned red-faced when they drank, like they had severe sunburns, and got quite verbal, so it was an entertaining sight. I swear there were nights they drank 30 or 40 beers, and it made for interesting 3:30 AM wakeup calls, with guys still completely drunk, dizzy and wobbling as they ran along the beach. One by one, they'd dash away into the bushes or behind the dunes to puke, running back into formation with the rest of us like nothing had happened. I must admit that I spent a time or two in those bushes, as well!

We concluded the morning sessions at the summer camp with jumping squats, and many, many punches, kicks, and blocks. I remember that we would continue our morning session every day until just before sunrise, at which time all 300 of us would leave the water for the beach. Just as the sun rose, the teacher would yell out *seiza shite dashite!* ("sit in kneeling position and straighten your posture") and we would kneel in *seiza* with our fists tightly closed on top of our thighs and our torsos and heads bolt upright, at which stage he would then yell *mokuso!* ("close your eyes and meditate"). Here we would stay for at least 15 to 20 minutes each morning, with our eyes closed, while the sun rose. I personally couldn't help but sneak open my eyes and take a peek at the beautiful sunrise, every now and then. I'm sure everybody else was doing the same. It was always so freezing when we started, but after five minutes of exercise we didn't even notice the cold, and we were all inspired to train in such a beautiful, pure natural setting.

I remember this camp for yet another reason, besides the fact that we had some of the most famous fighters ever training with us. Sosai was always a huge fan of sumo, and to break up the training one day, he decided to hold a sumo competition – which was fun, but taken very seriously by all the participants. I was putting on muscle and reasonably solid by this stage – about 172 pounds (78 kg) – and I thought I did pretty well, winning my first three sumo bouts in a row. But then I faced a hulk of a Japanese fighter, who literally rushed me and threw me straight out of the ring onto my back. It was a knockout tournament, so that was the end of my sumo "career."

There was a strong fighter named Masashi Kimoto, who represented Japan four years earlier in the World Championships, where he gave Andy Hug (a famous Swiss fighter and K-1 Kickboxing legend) a good run for his money. Kimoto wasn't fighting this year, but still came as a student to train at the camp. He was very strong in the sumo challenge, and was easily winning his bouts. He won his fifth, sixth, seventh and eighth bouts, and Sosai at this stage paused and said, "If you win two more bouts, you will represent Japan in the World Championship in November."

This blew everyone away, but if you really knew Sosai and knew how much he loved sumo, it wasn't such a huge surprise. Kimoto won his next bout, making it nine in a row, and then the pressure was really on. Then came the biggest sumo fight of his karate career, you could say. This sumo bout, surrounded by 300 screaming *karateka*, was going to be a turning point in his life.

He steadied himself, waited for the judge in the middle to yell *hajime* ("begin"), and raced out like a bull. Kimoto blitzed his opponent, slamming him to the sand for his 10th straight win, qualifying for the world tournament. I remember just how elated everyone was by his actions, and how all of us clapped and cheered and ran in and picked him up, throwing him in the air many times, yelling, screaming, and congratulating him.

Kimoto did go on to compete at the 1991 World Championship in November, doing well enough that he can definitely hold his head up high.

Winter camps were basically the opposite of the summer camps. Imagine swapping sand, surf, and sunshine for snow, cold icy roads, and freezing conditions. The winter camps were always held somewhere up north, and always close to waterfalls. Like the summer camps, they were held once a year, and students came from all over Japan to participate. Both summer and winter camps usually ran for about week.

In the winter camps we always had snow, and on the

second-to-last day we were expected to do a 13-mile half-marathon, running in our *gi*, with the same 13-mile run each year for all three years of my *uchi deshi* time. I could never understand why the Japanese dragged their feet on the way down the hill, and I was always in the top five. I remember Kuruda was a great runner, and he won at least two of the three years.

The last day, we would go to a freezing cold waterfall and stand under it only in our *gi* bottoms, and take turns doing some basic *kihon* or basic punches. As I've said, these camps, although they had some very tough challenges, were more about bonding than anything else.

The one winter camp I remember the most was my last winter camp, in January 1993, when on the second-to-last day it was snowing an absolute blizzard. This was the day that was scheduled for the 13-mile run, and I really thought they might call it off. It was 6.5 miles down a winding beautiful mountain, at the top of which was our camp headquarters, and then the 6.5 miles back up to the top, which was going to be the killer.

Northern Japan is famous for its steep mountains and excellent snow and skiing, so when it snowed, it *really* snowed, and the temperature fell well below zero. Parts of the mountain road were extremely steep, and I remember we had to be very careful not to slip and fall off the side of the mountain as we ran down.

I was a pretty good runner in those days, and being *uchi deshi*, we were always expected to lead the way. I remember in all three winter camps, I was always the first one to reach the bottom of the mountain. Going back up the mountain was, as you can imagine, 10 times harder. It made the run down seem like a stroll in the park. So there I was, running back up, and I found myself being overtaken by Kuruda and another Japanese I can't remember. The Pink Panther was just behind me, and Nick not too far behind him. I would like to say we were encouraging each other back up the hill, but it was a competition, and we were pushing ourselves to our utter limits, so there was literally no talking all the way back up – just pain and heavy breathing.

We were in sections hundreds of yards apart, and it was tough and lonely. When I got to the finish line, there was Kuruda and the other Japanese guy, and I was absolutely exhausted. I congratulated Kuruda and the other runner. We said *osu* to each other, and then I was waiting for the other *uchi deshi* to come back up. Next came the Pink Panther and a few other Japanese, and then Nick – at least in the top 10, which was also a magnificent effort. We only left once all the *uchi deshi* had finished, and went back to the camp as a team. I thought about how completely exhausted I was, and we all looked at each other, saying the same thing with our eyes as we made our way back to the camp's change rooms, slipping into the luxury of the hot Japanese *onsen*. I remember feeling on top of the world, sitting in this hot bath of water, and thinking that even a torturous run could be endured if this was the reward.

There is a lot of stuff on the internet that people often see from these winter camps, which have became quite famous around the world, and which others have often tried to repeat – particularly the standing under waterfalls whilst punching and blocking (kicking is too dangerous). If you've taken note of what I've just told you about the cold conditions of the run, and this year in particular, you can imagine how cold it was under the waterfall the next day! To be honest, I'm surprised no one ever came down with a severe case of hypothermia, but we were young, fit guys in those days, and the Japanese are known for their resilience and have that "never give up" spirit. But thank God for that *onsen!*

CHAPTER 36
CHANGES IN THE CAST

若獅子

Ligo had to go back home to America in his second year because of a visa issue, and he was gone for two months. By the time he came back, just after the World Championship in 1991, Nick and I were training harder and getting much stronger. I'd trained nonstop, and had been pretty lucky with injuries – the only thing that could derail you. I'd broken ribs and my thumb, but had just worked through those. I had avoided really terrible injuries, like when Nick snapped his shin. Still, it was hard to measure your own progress, so when foreign fighters went away for several months and then came back, they remarked how much my technique and fitness had improved and how powerful I was. For some reason, however, when Ligo came back he seemed to have changed, bringing a more cocky attitude with him. What had happened to him back in the U.S., I don't know.

When he returned to Japan, for the first week or so he kept mouthing off about being the best. Perhaps during his time in the U.S. he had told people about what he was doing, and talked himself into believing he was something special, rather than just a second-year *uchi deshi* like the rest of us. Regardless, somehow he had changed. It all came to a head one day when I had a verbal argument with him in the foyer before a class.

In the class, first Nick sparred with him, and even though Nick hadn't been part of that argument, he was also tiring of Ligo's cocky attitude. During the sparring, Nick clipped him in the face with a simple roundhouse kick, and Ligo automatically stopped fighting and walked to the mirror to see if his face was OK. This may seem normal in other sports, but not in a

Kyokushin Karate dojo – and particularly not in the den of the Young Lions. Ligo was a second-year senior, and having a first-year clip him, even with enough force so that he may have chipped a tooth, was something that was to be ignored with a typical Kyokushin poker face and fighting spirit. To walk over to the mirror and check your face was just not done, and to show weakness to a junior was completely unacceptable.

I was teaching this particular class, and I was shocked and disappointed and even ashamed that a senior would show such weakness in front of his junior. It just so happened that I was in line to be his opponent for the next fight, and I decided to go hard to show my displeasure. I didn't want to hurt or humiliate him, but I really thought that he should have shown greater toughness and spirit than he had.

I went hard at Ligo with a lot of body punches and kicks, and after about 20 seconds I dropped him. It wasn't unusual to dole out this sort of conditioning, but it was unusual for a student – particularly an *uchi deshi* – to crumble like this. He dropped to the dojo floor, and although he got up after a few seconds, his spirit was obviously broken and he wasn't going to continue.

After class, down in the basement where there were the showers and change rooms, Ligo broke down in tears and asked, "Why did you do this to me, Judd?" I didn't talk about the fact that his showing weakness to Nick, his junior, was what set me off, but I just told him it was part of training and that he should toughen up if he were to improve and get stronger. Remember: I was copping this every day, myself, from the likes of The Razorback and The Barber and all the other strong fighters from other dojos who came to the *Honbu* – especially for the black belt classes – and by now this sort of hard sparring was becoming the norm. Ligo didn't reply to me. He just got changed, remained quiet, and returned to the dormitory.

To be honest, I didn't think too much more of this until the following morning when I woke up to find Ligo missing from his futon. At first I thought he must have gone to training in the park early, but then when he didn't return for breakfast we thought perhaps he had been hit by a car while running, and we went looking for him. After a day of searching we went back to the dorm and realized all his belongings were gone, too, so we gathered he must have got up in the middle of the night and left.

Sosai Oyama never said a word about this, ever. Although he often told the Japanese students to be kind to us westerners, as we were so far away from our families, he never said anything about Ligo's disappearance.

We only found out weeks later that Ligo had written a letter to Sosai Oyama, and through his secretary, Ulrika, we found out he had gone back home to America. We were never told the reasons, but I can only assume that Nick and I giving him a hiding in the dojo must have had some effect, or at least been the straw that broke the camel's back. But for whatever reason, his heart and his head just weren't in it at that time.

Ligo came from a non-Kyokushin background, and not only did he fail to adapt his fighting style, he never tried to understand the Japanese mentality – and more importantly, the mentality of the *uchi deshi*. For instance, Ligo would brag about how he could do a jumping spinning heel kick and knock an apple off someone's head. I never saw him do it, but I did see him do a flying side kick in a demonstration. He flew through the air, just like he said he would, and did hit and smash some tiles – but he also hit the poor *uchi deshi* holding the tiles. Of course Ligo was apologetic, but it never stopped him from being flashy.

Ligo was very skilled and had amazing potential, but refused to listen to anyone, and that probably hindered his evolution as a Kyokushin fighter. Kyokushin is based on the foundations of conditioning your body, perfecting power kicks and punches, and really focusing on strength and power above all else. But Ligo sometimes cared more about looking good. Sosai always said we should carry our heads low, our eyes high, be reserved in speech, and train our hardest. But even more than a year after entering the Young Lion's dormitory, Ligo hadn't switched his point-scoring style. Sosai Oyama did not call Kyokushin "the strongest karate" for nothing, and not everyone would be a Young Lion.

I look at things differently now. It must have been very difficult for Ligo to adapt to a completely new fighting style, and I realize that he must have been going through a really hard time in the program, or struggling with something else in his life. I just wish he had opened up and said something to me so I could have helped him. So I was thrilled to see him go on to great success later in life. Ligo now owns his own dojo in America, and I still wish him all the best. He is happy doing what he loves, and he is good at it.

I guess it makes me realize that the only people who succeed – in the Young Lions program, in the dojo, or, perhaps, at life – are those who are doing what they want, what makes them truly happy. We are the only ones that write our future, and if you want something bad enough, you make it happen no matter what limits you have or what obstacles are in front of you. But you have to fall in love with the hard work and the day-to-day grind, not just the glory of reaching the goal, in order to achieve your dreams. That is the secret!

CHAPTER 37
FAREWELL TO THE MAN THEY CALLED "MOKODOMO"

若獅子

"If you do not overcome your tendency to give up easily, your life will lead to nothing." –Sosai Oyama

An even bigger shock than Ligo leaving was what happened to Mohamad, my French *Senpai*, a few months later. Mohamad started a year before me, so he should have been the first foreigner to graduate as an *uchi deshi*.

The problem was that Mohamad was lazy. Or, if not lazy, then completely mentally disengaged. By the end of his last year, Mohamad was missing classes, not giving much effort in the sparring, and generally being lazy in training. He said the right things and never talked back, so he didn't have an attitude problem verbally, but by his third year you could tell he wanted out of Japan. He was incredibly gifted, but Sosai and his seniors (including The Ranger) warned him many times that he needed to step things up. I remember once he said to me that after his graduation, the Japanese could all kiss his ass. I remember being shocked by his attitude, and telling him, "Don't count your chickens before they hatch."

A month before his graduation, in mid-February 1992, I remember Matsui talking to him on the stairway of the *Honbu*. I was in the dojo doing some stretching, and Matsui Senpai approached and asked Mohamad if he knew the Japanese word *gaman*, meaning "to persist or get through." Mohamad responded yes, he did. This was clearly a pep talk, and coming straight from Matsui – Sosai's right hand man – meant it must have been serious. Matsui finished the conversation with "*Gambatte Kudasai!*" or "Keep fighting on."

A week later, all three of us foreigners were called up to Sosai's office randomly in the afternoon. So Nick, Mohamad and I all ran to the office. When we entered his office we yelled *osu* and *shitsureishimasu* and lined up in front of him in *fuda dachi,* or formal ready stance, as we stared at the back of his newspaper, waiting for him to finish and speak. Eventually, Sosai lowered the paper and said, in English, "Mohamad, I have warned you many times to train harder and harder, but you haven't listened, so you are leaving. Go back to the dorm, pack your bags, and go back to France." Sosai then dismissed us all without another word.

Mohamad immediately began crying as we walked back to the dorm. I didn't know what to say. He'd been warned many times by the instructors, seniors, and Sosai himself. But he chose to ignore everyone. The man the Japanese called "Mokodomo" should really have been the first foreigner to ever graduate as an *uchi deshi,* but he must have been completely burnt out. Like I said, the mental side of the training and conditioning was perhaps even harder than the physical. How else do you explain someone dedicating two years and 11 months of their life to a goal, then losing the spirit to continue, and getting expelled with less than a month left to go? It was insane, and we were all in shock, but Mohamad was too far gone and just wanted out, like a soldier with Post Traumatic Stress Disorder.

Suddenly, the sliding window between the *Honbu* and the dorm opened, but it was Kato, who announced that Nick and I were ordered back to Sosai's office. My heart was pounding and my throat constricting as we sprinted to his office, which seemed like a thousand steps. Was I next? But as soon as we entered, Sosai looked straight up at us and said, "Judd, say the *dojo kun,*" which I did perfectly. He then said, "Nick, say the *dojo kun,*" which Nick did, though not so well as he was still a first-year. Then he said, "You're both doing well, keep training hard, *osu* and on your way." I knew I wasn't going to get kicked out,

Farewell to the Man They Called "Mokodomo"

but as a young kid there is always some doubt. That doubt probably served me well, because after that, I picked up my training even harder, and made sure no one had a reason to be dissatisfied with me.

The attrition rate for *uchi deshi* was not good, to say the least. When I first joined there were nine first-years, two second-years, and two third-years. Each year, hundreds or even thousands from around Japan and the rest of the world applied to be one of Sosai's honored students, but only eight to 10 would be accepted. Even though these students had to be highly skilled at karate, pass rigorous tests, interviews and be highly recommended by their teachers, the attrition rate was incredible – as the paltry numbers of second- and third-years remaining attested. When a student left, it usually happened in the first couple of months – and in the middle of the night. If I had to do the math, with eight to 10 beginning and two graduating at the end of the three years, that means only one in four or five actually graduated.

My year broke the record for the number of students who completed the course. We started with nine, and eight graduated. Nick's year, on the other hand, started with nine and finished with two. It always happened the same way. We would wake up one day, and one of the *uchi deshi* would have slipped away into the night.

This was no ordinary training camp and no ordinary life; this was three years of the most brutal and hardcore training anyone could possibly imagine. Not only that, but we *uchi deshi* were thousands of miles away from our friends and loved ones, and the same could be said of the Japanese students as well.

In 1946, when Sosai resolved to do his three years of training in the mountains, even his own student Yashiro fled into the night after only six months. Sosai remained to keep training for a year in solitude. He mastered just about every physical test, but suffered from a black well of loneliness, so he returned to Tokyo after 18 months. But legend has it that he soon resolved to finish the full three years and went back to complete the remaining 18 months alone. He never gave up, and resolved to finish what he started no matter what the setbacks or obstacles – a true testament to the spirit of *Kyokushin*.

Looking back, perhaps Sosai intended things to be this way. Only the strongest were meant to survive this toughest of martial arts schools. But Sosai was as compassionate as he was strict and demanding. A few months after Mohamad had been banished from the program, I heard that Sosai contacted him back in France and offered him the chance to return and complete his last year. Mohamad declined. Starting as young as he did, at 17, perhaps it was just too much for him, mentally and emotionally, and coming back may have seemed an even bigger hurdle. Wherever you are in the world now, good luck, Mokodomo.

CHAPTER 38
100-MAN KUMITE, FIGHTS 60 THROUGH 70s

若獅子

It was about fight number 60 that I began to fight very poorly. For some stupid reason, I just stood there and I was copping unnecessary damage.

Nick had been giving me great advice, yelling: "Make yourself big, Judd, keep the long guard." By keeping a long guard, with my hands and arms further out, I'd try to keep my opponent at a distance instead of crunching smaller, creating an easier target and turning my boding into a punching bag.

Keeping my opponent at bay would also give me space to work with technique, not just power, and give me room to breathe. Despite how fatigued I felt, I wasn't even breathing heavy or gasping for air, and the 10-second breaks between rounds were all the rest I needed. All of my training and sprints up hills were paying off.

I tried to follow Nick's instructions to a tee, to stay composed and keep my distance, but sometimes that's easier said than done. They say that when you run out of stamina, that's when your technique goes out the window, and that's 100% true. I was getting sloppy, losing concentration. I remember Nick and Ned telling me to move to the side, to work my angles and not be a punching bag for no reason.

I tried to do a few leg sweeps and combinations, but they weren't working anymore, and my opponents only came on stronger.

In the first half, nothing penetrated through my body, but suddenly I felt this weight and cloudiness entering my mind. Suddenly, my sweat-soaked *gi* felt like a 50-pound weight vest. Pushing down the seeds of panic that were budding in my mind, I tried to do a few spinning heel kicks to go for quick knockouts – mostly out of frustration, because nothing else was working. But instead of connecting I missed, my leg cutting into the air and sending me falling clumsily to the ground, my elbows crashing hard into the floor. This zapped my energy even more, and I struggled just to get back up. I wasn't fighting so smart anymore.

About fight number 70 things started rapidly deteriorating, as my deepest fear appeared: my legs started to cramp up. I didn't tell my support team because I didn't want to worry them (and there was nothing they could do to help me, anyway). But the cramping became so bad during the fights in the late 70's that I had to grit my teeth and use all of my focus just not to fall over and collapse. I was hobbling, couldn't kick, and at one stage had trouble even walking.

My opponents surely must have seen my first signs of fatigue. Weakness is the worst thing you can show your opponents, because they feed on it, becoming more bold and confident. Slowly, my deepest fears and about what might go wrong began to manifest.

There was no time-out like you have in other sports, where you can stretch the cramp out. I just had to live with it.

If anyone who has had severe leg cramps can attest, not being able to sit or stretch them out is like torture. As the fighters kept smashing punches into me, my upper body still felt strong and didn't hurt. But my legs were in excruciating pain and completely useless. Even a two-minute time-out would have made a world of difference, but if I paused or stopped for any reasons I would have been automatically disqualified from the 100-man *kumite*.

I remember going over to my corner in between fights and they asked me why I wasn't kicking, so I told them my legs were cramping severely, letting out some choice curse words. This surprised even me, because it's not something I do during tournaments or in a dojo, as I always try to maintain respect, but the pain was making me really unravel mentally.

Nick gave me some sound advice: "Do what you can do, Judd. You can still punch, so punch."

So that's what I did. I punched like my life depended on it. The cramping wouldn't cease at all as I fought on, and I had 25 fights to go, so there was nothing I could do but get real comfortable in hell.

CHAPTER 39
FRIENDSHIP, RIVALRY AND CRUELTY IN THE DOJO

若獅子

"Human beings are capable of virtually limitless degradation; they are also capable of virtually limitless improvement and achievement. Success depends on goals and on diligence in pursuing them."
–Sosai Oyama

In my second year in as an *uchi deshi*, in 1991, there were a lot of changes in the Young Lion's dormitory – some for the good, and some for the bad.

Starting my second year, I was no longer a foot soldier or private but now the equivalent of, say, a corporal in the army, and I had a lot more freedom. My new ally, Nick, had arrived from Denmark, and although he was my junior, I mostly abandoned formality outside of training and treated him as the good mate he was. This was about the time the Pink Panther decided to come out of his shell, too, now that he was no longer squeezed in the vice of discipline that first-years were.

Just like his nickname suggests, the Pink Panther was one smooth, cool cat. He didn't care about anything, or about what anyone thought of him – very unusual for a Japanese. He would do everything that was asked of him in the dojo, and come back for more. He was tough as nails while training or sparring, but also had a great sense of humor, which he could now unleash on the world. So by my third year, the Pink Panther, Nick, and I became the Three Musketeers of the Young Lions. There weren't a lot of deep and personal friendships among the other Japanese *uchi deshi* – that just wasn't their way. They didn't engage in lighthearted interactions or share encouragement from day to day, but preferred to remain understated and stoic, valuing mastery over their emotions and blending into the greater organization or system above all else. But the camaraderie among Nick, the Pink Panther and I couldn't have been stronger, and my friendships with those guys really made the last two years enjoyable.

The Pink Panther was the perfect first-year – an obedient foot soldier *uchi deshi* – but you could see there was something waiting to break loose after he had his first year as a slave behind him. I got to know Yamagaki even better as we lifted weights a lot together in the basement, starting in the second year. The Pink Panther was nice to his juniors, and in the dojo he always gave 100%. I think he was a green belt before he became an *uchi deshi,* because he was just too good to have never trained before. (Sosai Oyama frequently took lower ranked students who he thought had potential and a fire in their belly because it was much easier to teach and mold someone who hadn't developed bad habits yet.)

Suzuki, as I said, bossed everyone around and was always confrontational – even with his equals. He was the same year as the Pink Panther and I, but always tried to tell us what to do. I remember the Pink Panther and him went over to the park around November of the first year and had a punch-on one time, to sort out their differences. Suzuki was trying to be the bigwig, as usual, and although the Pink Panther had to take this from his seniors, he didn't need to take it from his equal. Both Suzuki and the Pink Panther came back covered in bruises on their faces. I don't know who won, but that was the last time Suzuki tried to boss him around again. The Pink Panther and Suzuki were about the same level in first year, but by second and third year my good friend and training partner had pulled far ahead.

In third year the Pink Panther was doing a lot of weights, and he used to roll up his t-shirt sleeves and walk around the dormitory to show off his muscles. By third year he had long

Friendship, Rivalry and Cruelty in the Dojo

hair and he would shave it at the sides, *yakuza* style. (Of course first-year *uchi deshi* had to shave their heads – which wasn't yet common in the 1990s – but second- and third-years could grow it out and wear it as they liked.)

I even have a picture of the Pink Panther giving the bird, which was shocking and rare for a Japanese in those days. He didn't give a damn. He looked like a cartoon character, and even at times when he was drunk – when we were allowed out to local *izakaya* every few months to eat and drink beer – he would put an unlit cigarette in his mouth and don a pair of old-school sunglasses and act like a full-power *yakuza*.

I remember in our third year, when the three of us were closest, he used to sit around teaching Nick and I street Japanese – a way of speaking that you generally only saw in Beat Takeshi movies, a famous Japanese director notorious for making *yakuza* films. The Japanese language has an incredible system of manners, grammar, and particular way of talking, depending on whom you are communicating with. There is very polite Japanese reserved for customers in shops, polite Japanese reserved for your seniors and elders, street Japanese that is spoken between friends, and then *yakuza*-style Japanese that would scare the crap out of an ordinary person. The Pink Panther thought it was funny to teach Nick and me the way a *yakuza* would talk. Soon, both Nick and I sounded like Japanese mafia, using words and phrases that no ordinary foreigner knew. If we wanted to, we could sound like full-power mafia with the perfect accent, thanks to the Pink Panther.

Another gangster mannerism of the Pink Panther's, which I never saw anywhere else in Japan, took place when we were eating in the dining room. He would stick both of his chopsticks facing downward into the rice bowl, which signifies death in Japanese, and then go into full-on *yakuza* mode. In second year he would do it with a mocking smile when there were no seniors present, but by third year he was the senior, so he did it and yelled a few *yakuza* phrases to add to the character he was playing and shock the younger Japanese students. Don't get me

197

wrong; he was not a bad guy, by any means. He was always kind to his juniors and showed respect to his seniors, but to Nick and I, he was and always will be the Pink Panther. Not many people know about these things, but it kept us amused and helped break up the monotony of the dorm.

1991 also saw the entrance of Taichiro Sugimura, who Nick and I nicknamed The Razorback for two reasons. The first was that he was a 220-pound (100 kg), 5'11" beast of a human being – preternaturally strong, with excellent technique. He had even beaten many famous Japanese fighters, including Hiroki Kurosawa, who was the All Japan champion in 1984 and came third in the last world tournament.

The other reason we named Sugimura after a wild boar was because it sometimes seemed he was more animal than human. He was similar to The Ranger, but a lot stronger, more dominating, and he felt nothing about bashing students in the dojo at whim. In fact, I would say he punched harder than anyone I've ever seen. Moreover, it seems he took pleasure in bashing people, though I wouldn't say he was anti-foreigner – he was an equal opportunity basher of anyone and everyone. The Razorback hurt them with his powerful body punches and then wrecking ball thigh kicks, making sure they couldn't walk right for weeks. To be on the receiving end of one of his hidings, particularly if you were smaller or less experienced than he was, was not a particularly pleasant experience.

The Razorback wasn't an *uchi deshi,* but from my second year onward, he trained pretty much every day of the week and was well respected in the dojo for being so tough and strong. I heard that he came from Akira Masuda's dojo – the 1990 All Japan champion – so it seemed fitting that he was a super strong *karateka.* Aside from the fact that The Razorback was unusually large-framed for a Japanese, he seemed to almost have a twin personality. He would come to the *Honbu* in a suit after work, wearing these thick coke-bottle glasses. He was all *osu, hai* and *shitsureishimasu* until he put on his *dogi* and stepped onto the *Honbu* training floor. This is when he went into

Razorback mode – like a Japanese version of the Incredible Hulk.

It has been said by many over the years that the *Honbu* and particularly the *uchi deshi* course is like a modern-day version of a gladiator school. If that's true, then The Razorback was the epitome of that tough, mean gladiator who would sort out the men from the boys. If you could take a bashing from The Razorback and survive, you probably were going to get through this. If you couldn't take a bashing – or at least find a way to get stronger and more conditioned to be able to take that sort of punishment – your chances of getting through the whole three years diminished greatly.

The Razorback was about four or five years older than me, was a second-degree black belt, and as I said he became a regular on the scene during my second year onwards and was a force to reckoned with.

By my third year, The Razorback decided to start his own fighting squad – of which he was in charge. The senior *uchi deshi* were automatically expected to join, and this intensified the training immensely. In total, The Razorback's fighting squad had 15 members, about five of which were *uchi deshi* and the other 10 were *soto deshi*. The aim of this squad was to produce fighters of the caliber that would be able to compete on a world-class level in All Japan and World Tournaments. This class was held twice a week, without the normal teachers (it was run by The Razorback, and we didn't even wear our *gi* – perhaps shorts and t-shirts or just *gi* pants). It was held on the ground floor in the smaller dojo, and with little natural ventilation it could be unbearably hot and humid in the summer time. I remember The Razorback would call out for cold *mugicha* (tea) during the class, and one of the junior *uchi deshi* standing at attention at the front door would run out and prepare it for us mid-class during the breaks.

In these squad classes, we'd do an hour of hard bag work and punching, kicking, and technical drills – and then it was really time to get down, with sparring.

We'd pair off, but I remember I ended up fighting The Razorback most times. We'd start off fighting at about 50 percent, like the rest of the fighters. He was looking for openings and trying to set up combinations so he could smash into me with his powerful thigh kicks.

I knew that he was trying to take me down with those thigh kicks, but I didn't care – I knew I could take it and come back with just as much punishment.

Our fight would quickly escalate far past light sparring, and soon we were going at each other 100%. I would focus on trying to smash right through his thighs, aiming to finish my follow-through on the other side of his femur, and mixed it up by trying to land a high, descending axe kick down onto his skull. The Razorback kicked my inside leg hard and followed up with ferocious knees to my body that pushed me back.

But I wasn't about to give an inch, so I'd counter by whipping a thunderous roundhouse kick straight into his ribs, the sound of bone on bone echoing through the whole room.

The Razorback and I were seriously trying to kill each other, going at it with 100% ferocity, every punch and kick thrown with extreme prejudice.

Afterwards, we'd just bow to each other and go one with our day, like nothing had happened. These were the sessions where you'd really get your gains. Of course I'd leave The Razorback's fight squad sessions with bumps and bruises on my shins, ribs and hands, but that was nothing compared to two years earlier as a new *uchi deshi*, when I was battered and barely able to walk after each session. I'd come a long way in two years.

My body had grown much stronger. My shins were calcified, my legs felt like oak tree trunks, and even my ribs had calcified after cracking and healing so many times. My body felt like a coat of unbreakable armor. It was a great feeling, and I had to thank The Razorback and others for these epic do-or-die fighting sessions.

People often say that the best sparring is seen in the dojo

when the outside world isn't watching, and I would definitely agree.

Even though The Razorback was a tough guy – and, perhaps, looking back he was a bit of a bully in the dojo – Nick and I really benefited a lot from his presence. I have to say, he really toughened the two of us up, and in some way prepared us for the lifetime of punishment that awaits the professional fighter.

In any case, I had a certain amount of respect for The Razorback. He was here on a mission to be the best he could, and he liked to fight, but his ferocity started and ended with the classes. He was not the cruel, spiteful bully like The Ranger, who disliked the other *uchi deshi* and got pleasure in dishing out torture to his *kohai*. In my second year, The Ranger really began to step up his cruelty, and with the arrival of nine new first-years, he had a whole new list of victims to yell at, abuse, and make do jumping squats in the park all night.

People often think that the Japanese must have given us foreigners a terrible time, but to be honest, that really wasn't the case. Sosai, to his credit, often told the Japanese that we foreigners had it hard, being so far from our families, so they should help us out. I wouldn't say they made it easy for us, and they definitely tried to assert their superiority in the dojo, but to be honest Nick and I improved very quickly, and by the time we both reached our second year we could hold our own with just about anyone in the dojo. Sosai was impressed enough that he had me teaching classes from second year, which was extremely rare. In fact, I don't know of any other second-years who ever taught classes except Nick, also in his second year.

To be honest, if there was any cruelty to be seen, it was mostly Japanese on Japanese. This was really a *Senpai/kohai* (senior/junior) thing, and to an outsider it may have seemed very cruel, but to me it just part of the *uchi deshi* system. But sometimes, things did go too far, no matter who you were or where you were from.

One time I walked into the dining room and saw Ishida, a

second-year at the time and acting as Sosai's driver, in a handstand against the wall. Hashimoto, a third-year, was kicking him in the guts as hard as he could for some minor infraction and yelling *bakayaro,* or "you idiot." I never worked out the exact reason, but no matter what he did, it seemed overly cruel punishment. All the while Ishida was getting kicked and yelled at, he would scream back *osu* and *shitsreishimatshita* as was to be expected by a *kohai*. It went on for at least half an hour and reverberated through the whole *Honbu* dormitory. Robo San, funnily enough, was in the kitchen cooking through all of this and ignored it completely.

When the Japanese went off like that against each other, everyone would ignore it – an unspoken code among them – and just pretend it wasn't happening. It may seem strange now, but it was normal back then.

Knowing that Ishida was Sosai's driver, I actually wondered if his bruises would have been seen by Sosai, and if there would be any repercussions, but I never heard anything about it again. Ishida may not have been the sharpest of the *uchi deshi,* but he always tried his best and gave everything 100%, so to this day I wonder what he must have done wrong to cop such a beating.

Ishida, Kumokai, and Suzuki were the only three of the *uchi deshi* in my year that had never trained Kyokushin before they started. Applicants had to write a letter and go through a series of tests. It was mostly about attitude and inner strength, which Sosai was looking for. All three graduated in the end, so I guess they were made of the right stuff.

As Sosai's driver, Ishida rarely had any free time, always at the beck and call of Sosai, who expected him to exhibit extreme punctuality, discipline, and complete respect. This treatment wasn't just for Sosai, but for anyone traveling with or greeting Sosai at the beginning and end of each journey. The pressure on Ishida must have been enormous. I remember one time we were having a nap up in the dorm, about half an hour before Sosai's Thursday *uchi deshi* class, trying to get some rest before it began. Ishida had a watch on, and his alarm went off. He turned off his alarm and sure enough, about three minutes later his alarm went off again. He kept falling asleep after each alarm, for a grand total of three minutes each time. Incredibly this went on for an entire 30 minutes. Trying to get some rest myself, I was annoyed, but I knew he had incredible responsibilities so I said nothing.

When we saw someone being treated unfairly or abused, Nick and I had our own way of doling out justice where we thought justice was due. Ishida was never the strongest of the *uchi deshi*, nor were a few of the others, but if we saw them bullied or picked on, we placed it in our memory bank and made sure that when it came time to fight in the dojo, we settled the score.

But Nick and I could only do so much, I guess, and protecting the Japanese from the mental bullying of the likes of The Ranger was just not possible. He was a senior teacher, and always avoided sparring me in the classes he took, but it wouldn't be long before he turned his attentions toward Nick and I in a completely unexpected manner.

CHAPTER 40
NICK'S GRADING

若獅子

"1-2 out of every 100 students reach black belt, and of those only 1 out of every 1,000 achieves his second dan." –Sosai Oyama

Nick went for his black belt grading at the end of March of his first year in 1992. This was almost unheard of for a first-year student, as everyone (except me) had to start as a white belt. When Nick left Demark he was a brown belt, only one step away from black belt. To be considered for your black belt second *dan* you usually had to have 30 fights under your belt and be a senior, but he was so far ahead of the other *uchi deshi* in his year that Sosai insisted that Nick should go for his black belt grading; quite an honor.

A brown belt who is going for his black belt would have to fight 10 people to earn it, but usually at least 30 people would be going for their grading, and there would be some breaks between the fights. Nick, however, was made to stand up in front of the class so Sosai could say a few words about his grading in particular. I remember he said that he was very proud of Nick, and that this was an unusual case, but Nick was going to sit his black belt on this day and do 10 consecutive fights. Fighting consecutively like that was very unusual, but he instructed all of the fighters to go against Nick as hard as they could. He glanced toward Nick and said, "Give it your best and fight hard, and try to knock them all down." He also said – to our utter amazement – "Nick, if you get seven knockouts, I will award you not your first *dan* but your second *dan* today."

He then said something that shocked us even more, adding, "If you knock down all 10 fighters, I will give you your third *dan.*"

Nick yelled *osu gambarimasu* ("I will give it my best shot") in a very loud and clear voice.

I was alone in Nick's corner, and so the fights began in the center of the *Honbu* dojo. Now, anyone who is familiar with a Kyokushin grading knows that before this, the student has already done all their *kihon* (basics) and *kata* (patterns), and the final challenge is the fighting. So, with probably 40 fighters, spectators, and officials present in the completely packed *Honbu* dojo, Nick's fights began.

I remember saying to Nick, "You can do this. Pick your shots and hurt them."

Nick was fighting all the brown belts going for their black belts that day. Basically, Nick steamrolled the first four fighters, knocking each of them down with a combination of axe kicks, back spinning heel kicks, and dropping them with powerful thigh kicks and body shots. It was looking like Nick was going to do this easily, and I was going to have him as a fellow second *dan* within a few more minutes of fighting. Sosai was applauding Nick's efforts and nodding with approval, and he actually told the Japanese to step it up and fight even harder.

So I remember during Nick's fifth and sixth fights, the Japanese gave their absolute all, and the fights were a draw and another draw. At this stage I thought, "Well, at least he won't be my senior after this!"

The seventh fight, he knocked out the fighter, so the second *dan* was still on. The eighth fight was another draw; the ninth was incredibly close, but just pipped for a draw. The very last fight, Nick absolutely smashed his opponent, knocking him down, but unfortunately, it was only his sixth knockout – a cruel twist that left him just one shy of the target set by Sosai for his second *dan*.

Despite this, Sosai was extremely proud, and I think perhaps secretly surprised that he had come so close. At the end of his fights, Nick went over to Sosai and shook both his hands, and bowed down low as per normal, and Sosai gave him a strong pat on the back saying, "*Tsubarashi, Nicholasu, tsuyoi yo, sugoi yo,*" ("Wonderful, Nick, you are strong, very, very strong!") and Nick went and sat back down amongst the other students grading as a freshly minted black belt.

CHAPTER 41
IKEBUKURO AND THE YAKUZA

若獅子

The *Honbu* dojo is located at the west exit of Ikebukuro train station. Anyone who knows Tokyo knows that part of the city is full of love hotels, snack bars and hostess bars. It also happens to be a huge *yakuza*, or Japanese mafia, enclave. The *Honbu* dojo is a couple of miles south of this area, and is in a fairly quiet part of the neighborhood next to a small park. In fact, in those days the *yakuza* actually had one of their main offices in Ikebukuro, complete with a big gold-plated sign announcing the organization, and two armed guards in suits and sunglasses stationed out front.

We as *uchi deshi* had nothing to do with these guys. They worked as bouncers at casinos and hostess bars in the red light districts of Tokyo, and were involved in protection, gambling, and just about every shadowy racket in the city. You could always spot a *yakuza*; they wore black suits with crisp white shirts and black ties, mirrored sunglasses even at night, and drove jet-black shiny Mercedes to match. Many of the *yakuza* had elaborate tattoos that sometimes covered their entire bodies from their necks all the way down to their ankles, but usually only under the shirt line so they could try to blend in. I remember the *yakuza* wearing a certain kind of scarf in the wintertime and carrying stylish man bags under one arm instead of wallets. They walked with a swagger, a side-to-side strut that was hard to miss, as if they were marking their territory, though they didn't bother average citizens. If that wasn't enough to spot a *yakuza*, you only had to look at their hands. If a *yakuza* made a mistake or bungled a job or mission, their finger would be chopped off as an act of attrition and a token of their renewed loyalty. I would see guys with two or even three or four fingers missing at the knuckles, starting with their pinkies and working in. This wasn't torture or a form of punishment, because no one had to hold down the *yakuza* and do this to them – they would cut their own fingers off with a sharp knife in front of their bosses.

Of course, I'm sure that the *yakuza* all knew of Sosai Oyama and his dojo on the other side of the west exit, but they showed us mutual respect and left us alone. However, the area they controlled often had trouble at night, and was generally avoided by us students.

I remember one time the Pink Panther and Oshikiri came back to the dojo with bruises on their faces, and the police had been involved. The story went that they encountered a large number of Russian gangsters who started trouble with them. These older thugs probably thought they could pick on these two young Japanese kids because there were six of them. I can only imagine their reaction when Pink Panther and Oshikiri – who by this time were third-years – unleashed a fury of punches and kicks on them!

In contrast to his famous sense of humor and ability to make us fellow *uchi deshi* fall down laughing at his antics, the Pink Panther was also one tough mother. He had a take-no-crap and fear-nothing attitude, and by third year, he walked around with this air of confidence and invincibility. I guess those thugs had no idea what they were in for that day!

I heard from the Pink Panther that they absolutely smashed the six gangsters, despite being outnumbered. Of course neither Oshikiri nor he were' looking for trouble and they didn't start it, but they sure did finish it. By the end there were half a dozen Russian bodies on the ground, unconscious or moaning in pain. But the Pink Panther and Oshikiri didn't come out unscathed; they each had visible bruises on their faces when they made it back to the dojo, though it was nothing worse than they received from time to time in training.

The Pink Panther and Oshikiri made the mistake of hanging

around the area after the fight was over ("to collect trophies," we called it!), and some bystanders called the police. Sosai had to be called to resolve the situation. Clearly the Pink Panther and Oshikiri were just defending themselves, and against bigger guys and superior numbers, so the police took all of this into account and neither side pressed charges. One thing I do remember clearly was Sosai Oyama dressing them down – not for fighting or defending themselves, but asking why they waited around for the police.

Sosai's teachings may have been rooted in philosophies about life and the martial way, but this showed that he was also a very practical, streetwise man. As I've said, he told us many old war stories of fighting in his younger days, and often said to us, "You are learning karate to be able to fight well in a street fight," so he had no problem with us defending ourselves like this. His words were: "Smash these guys, don't hang around, and don't get caught by the police." This is probably the only time I remember the *uchi deshi* fighting outside of the tournaments or dojo, but a story I remember clearly.

I had heard stories from Wada's days about the reason why there were always two *uchi deshi* on guard at the front of the dojo. Apparently there was quite a bit of rivalry between the various karate organizations even up to a few years before I got there. Perhaps Sosai Oyama declaring Kyokushin Karate "the strongest karate" put a few noses out of joint? I can't remember who told me this, but I heard it more than once, and I'm sure it happened. The story was that members of other dojos would go around to rivals' dojos and try to invade and get in punch-ons with those dojos to prove who was really stronger. One story was that it had happened right out in front of the *Honbu* and involved about 20 or 30 intruders, and the whole dojo poured out and a huge fight ensued in the street right out front. The story didn't make clear the details of who actually won or lost, although I'm sure the *Honbu* guys won, and perhaps Sosai decided to keep this story to himself as it was a little too close to home. But it certainly explained the presence of the two *uchi deshi* guards at the front, from that time onward.

CHAPTER 42
SUZUKI AND ME, DUELING IT OUT

若獅子

I've already told you that Suzuki was hardcore Japanese, very strict, and ex-army. Six feet tall and a strong fighter, he wanted to be the boss and rule his fellow first-year students, and still thought that by the time we all reached third-year.

One time in our second-year, in November at the 1991 World Tournament, there was an incident I remember clearly. At the end of the tournament, all of us *uchi deshi* who were there had to pack up the mats and clean up. I was talking to the Australian team and being diplomatic, as was expected of us foreign *uchi deshi*, to make the visiting teams feel comfortable. However, Suzuki came over and gave me a huge blasting in front of everyone, talking in very disrespectful Japanese, not caring who heard or viewed this extremely demeaning behavior. My blood was boiling, but rather than fuel the fire and further disrespect our dojo and master, I finished my conversation with the Australian team. They didn't understand what it was all about, except that his aggressive and disrespectful demeanor was obvious. After I finished my chat with the Aussies, I politely excused myself to complete my duties, but logged the incident in my memory for a later date.

About six months later we third-years were training outside, doing our conditioning in front of the *Honbu*. By this stage we were both getting incredibly strong, having trained solidly for almost two and a half years. So that morning we began by thigh kicking each other in turn without checking, which was a usual practice for conditioning the legs, so that you'd become used to that in a tournament.

I happened to be matched up with Suzuki, my blowhard tormentor. We stepped it up to a medium pace, which was also not so unusual, but I could see on his face that he wanted to prove a point. He continued to kick me harder until we were close to full intensity, and I'm sure he thought I could take no more and would show weakness and break. Before long we were not only kicking but also punching each other, no holds barred, at full power and both trying to keep our best poker face expressions. By this stage I'd put on a lot of weight and had been doing a lot of weight training, and had really transformed from that skinny kid I was in first-year at 145 pounds (65 kg) to about 188 pounds (85 kg). Suzuki, on the other hand, was taller than me, and only about 158 pounds (72 kg), but also very strong.

Standing out in front of the *Honbu* and literally smashing each other, the hits were making a huge repetitive thudding noise of *smack, smack, smack* and began to draw a crowd of other *uchi deshi* and also a number of part-time students – maybe 10 people in total. They had wide-eyed looks on their faces, and they were transfixed completely by what was occurring, forgetting their own drills and watching us instead. Perhaps they didn't understand the motivation for us trying to kill each other, but they knew some sort of score was being settled. And there was no way I was going to back down and give Suzuki the upper hand, not only over me but also over my fellow mates.

I could see that Suzuki was hanging in there, but he started to give a little wince whenever I connected, and that was the only chink in the armor I needed to know he was beginning to wear down. His eyes began to twitch and register pain, and his body started to cave in to absorb each shot. Since I was stronger and bigger than him, and also because I was fighting for pride, his blows were not having nearly the same effect on me. Once I noticed he was close to the breaking point, perhaps even buckling and falling, it registered in my head that this wouldn't be a proper display of etiquette in front our juniors. So I pulled up on my punches and kicks and we slowed it down until we both came to a stop. To his credit, he hung in there, and at the end we bowed to each other and said *osu* and parted ways, with neither of us losing face. But I knew that this was the turning point.

Later that day we had our weekly Sunday class with Sosai, and Suzuki was a mess. He was shaking and could barely even stand, let alone kick and punch, after taking such a beating. I looked at Sosai's expression, and you could tell he knew something was up. Normally if a black belt was wobbling around like human jelly, as Suzuki was, Sosai would have barked at him and asked what the hell was going on. But in this class he never said a word. I can only assume he had heard what had happened earlier in the day. Suzuki's dynamic and our relationship changed forever after this. Never again did he talk to me in a disrespectful manner, and from here until the end of my time as an *uchi deshi* he was always courteous, treating me as the equal I had become.

CHAPTER 43
THE RANGER MAKES HIS MOVE

若獅子

"Personal greed and egoism are things that cause human beings to forget respect for others and to violate rules that have been established for the sake of peace and friendship." –Sosai Oyama

    A confrontation with my biggest rival and the biggest bully in the *Honbu* – Yui Senpai, The Ranger – came a couple of months later at the yearly summer camp. I already told you he didn't like Nick and I, but the same could probably be said for all the other students, too. I'd had my run-in with Suzuki, but the difference between Suzuki and The Ranger was that Suzuki was a bossy rival, whereas The Ranger was just a cruel human being four to five years my senior who enjoyed inflicting pain on the helpless and weak.

    I was a third-year *uchi deshi,* and Nick a second-year, at the summer camp that August. We were called for a talk in the lobby of the Japanese inn where we were staying. It was an old style Japanese inn, and when we entered we saw that the room was empty except for The Ranger and his Swedish girlfriend, Ulrika, sitting down at a table. I was about eight months away from graduation, and I clearly remember him telling us to sit down in a loud and direct voice, as he had something important he needed to tell us. I had no idea what was coming next, but he had this very serious look on his face and had brought Ulrika along as a translator – even though, by this stage, we could understand 100% of his Japanese. I guess the point was that he didn't want whatever he was about to say to get lost in translation.

    The Ranger took his time before speaking, pausing to look

Nick and I up and down, before conveying to us his completely outrageous orders. He blurted out, "You two need to pack your bags and leave Japan. You are not worthy of even calling yourselves *uchi deshi!*" We were stunned, almost speechless. But before we could even protest, he repeated that our time as *uchi deshi* was over. He told us to immediately return to the *Honbu*, pack our bags, and go home.

We were both completely shocked by this. My initial response was, "Why?"

He said we weren't Japanese, weren't fitting in with traditional ways, and weren't pulling our weight in regards to chores. We couldn't do things like going to the bank, answering the phone at the *Honbu*, or do things that involved speaking lifelong Japanese, and he had a problem with that.

In our defense, I told him we trained harder and took more classes than the Japanese. That was a fact, and he knew it. But he still insisted that we should go back to the *Honbu*, pack our bags, and get out.

I collected myself and put my anger in check before I responded. "There's no way in hell that's happening," I told him in English, and then repeated it to Ulrika, his Swedish girlfriend (and Sosai's sometime secretary), so I was sure he understood. I grew angry with her, too. I understood 100% of what he saying in Japanese, but to have to hear Ulrika repeat these ridiculous orders just doubled the insult. I was boiling over furious he would even suggest it, let alone demand it.

Both Nick and I stood our ground, furiously staring them both down. We would not be intimidated one iota. I told him I disagreed with him, and was refusing his order. I told him that Nick and I were training harder than anyone else, and neither of us were leaving. Nick piped up as well, and said he wasn't leaving, either.

It was a good thing we were still sitting down, because the moment grew so intense that I felt it could escalate to a full on fight at any second, and I now Nick was thinking the same. God only knows what was going through Ulrika's head at this point,

The Ranger Makes His Move

and with all of the tension between us, she probably thought we would all jump up start brawling. The Ranger insisted, again, that we leave but I looked him dead on, my eyes blazing, and simply said "No." The thoughts in my head were more like: "There is just no way in hell!" Sosai had taught us to stand up to bullies and never back down, and I knew this order wasn't coming from him.

The Ranger was the first to blink. He paused and said something like, *"Ja sore da?"* or "Is that the way it is?" and I said steadfastly, "Yes, it is." Nick and I both took a step back, excused ourselves with the formal *shitsureishimasu,* and left the room biting my lip in anger. As we walked down the stairs and out of the building, shoulder to shoulder, I turned to Nick and said: "The next time we get into the dojo, I am going to knock him out."

Nick simply replied, "Damn straight, Judd!"

And that was that – or so I thought.

To this day, I still don't know why he chose that particular time to make this announcement, but to my utter amazement, a week later back at the *Honbu* he called the two of us together again – without Ulrika there to translate this time, and repeated the exact same spiel. But even worse, it was in the foyer of the *Honbu* on the ground floor – a very public place – and he was ordering us to leave in Japanese, without caring who overheard. I thought I couldn't have been more shocked. But to try this stunt again – and now with no concern as to who else might be listening – was an absolute insult. It's as if he was purposely trying to humiliate and dishonor us. I was so infuriated I had to take deep breaths so I didn't start smashing him to pieces right then and there. Nick and I waved him off and dismissed him quickly this time, repeating that there was no way we were leaving, walking away from him, and heading straight back to the dormitory.

All that mattered to me was that Sosai was proud of Nick and I, and the progress we were making, continuously encouraging us and even calling us his own children. I knew that The Ranger didn't represent Sosai's wishes or feelings in any way.

I'm sure the Ranger was the main reason the majority of the students in Nick's year abandoned the *uchi deshi* program in their first few months, with nine starting but only two graduating.

The Ranger seemed to think that Nick and I being there meant we took the place of another deserving Japanese, and you could just tell that it incensed him. I suspect what he disliked the most was that since we weren't Japanese, he couldn't get inside our heads and torture us like he did the other juniors. I was either going to get him back or show him why I was deserving of a place in the Young Lions. As it turned out, it wouldn't be long before I was able to prove my point – and there would be far less talking this time.

CHAPTER 44
THE 100-MAN KUMITE, FIGHTS 70 THROUGH 90

若獅子

By the fights in the late 70s to early 90s I thought my legs might snap off, the pain was so bad. I couldn't kick at all and I could barely move. I was getting punched and kicked like that heavy bag in the basement. I gazed straight towards my opponent, still trying to counter fight and make my shots count, but they weren't having the same effect at all.

But I was still determined to finish, even if it meant crawling on the ground to do it. That might sound silly, but I was prepared to put my life on the line – and that was a serious possibility, considering the state of shock my body was in.

I remember hearing fight number 90 yelled, and thought of gold at the end of the rainbow. There was nothing that was going to stop me.

Even my forearms were cramping up now, and my entire body – not just my legs – was in crippling pain. But I still wanted to win these fights, not to score points but somehow because my survival depended on it. I was fighting on natural instinct now, totally delusional.

Did my support team see that? I felt like I wasn't human, and totally withdrawn from reality. When I went back to my corner the guys would put ice on the back of my neck, which numbed some of my sizzled nerves and kept my core temperature from soaring to dangerous levels.

Nothing they were saying now was registering. Even the ice pack felt like a huge weight, but I was too delirious to say anything. I remember crouching over at one point. It was a bad move. It felt like I was going to hit the ground and never be able to stand back up again.

So I held my head high and went back in fighting, *kiai'*ing out loud and giving it everything I had. I managed to do a leg sweep somehow, dropping my surprised opponent to the ground. The crowd roared their approval, but I was too far gone to hear it.

CHAPTER 45
KING OF THE WORLD

若獅子

It wasn't common for the *uchi deshi* to fight in regional tournaments, as most of us didn't have much tournament fighting experience when we first began. We were still considered young trainees, but some of us improved a great deal by third-year so Sosai deemed us tournament-worthy. I remember the Pink Panther and Kuruda fighting in India in 1993, and they placed highly. In 1994, Kuruda and Suzuki fought in the lightweight division of the All Japan tournament and also placed very well.

As an *uchi deshi* I fought in the All Japan in first-year, but did no tournament fighting my second-year because it was thought I needed to get much stronger before reentering tournaments. But by my third-year I was invited to three big regional tournaments, which I gladly accepted and fought in all of them.

Tournaments were always an adrenaline rush for me. I never feared getting hurt. Fear was more about your doubts, but that fear maxed out about one week out. When I tried to sleep at night or had some down time I'd stare at the ceiling and think: have I done all the right preparation, have I done the right training, have I peaked at the right time? Being human, you can't help but have at least some doubts in your head. In my early years, I couldn't sleep the night before the tournament. I was anxious, and fearful of disappointing people and myself. I would have many things going through my mind. Only in my thirties, with all the experience of past tournaments, could I manage to sleep the night before. By then I had more control over my nerves and emotions, and I knew that creeping doubts and questions about whether I had trained hard enough were just a normal part of the process and would quickly go away.

My biggest fear, going into fights, was losing and looking bad and not doing myself proud. People may think of Judd Reid as this superman who has no fear, but I am human just like anyone else. But by learning to control our fear, we have the key to overcome it. Some fighters are superstars in the dojo but always have trouble in tournaments. Everyone is different. It is one thing to train and spar in the dojo, but if you want to win in tournaments, you have to love to fight. That is the biggest difference. The great ones, you could see it in their eyes that they wanted to *fight*, not just wanted to *win*. You have to love the game to play it right.

The first tournament I was invited to that year was the Tochigi Prefectural Tournament in July 1992. This tournament had weight divisions, and I fought in the heavyweight (over 175 pounds, or 80 kg) division. I had four fights, of which I won three – two by knockout. This was about two months before The Ranger told us we should pack up and leave. Can you believe it? I came in runner-up in a big regional tournament and proved that I belonged there and that my training was paying off, yet he still had the gall to say I didn't deserve my place.

Not long after the summer camp and The Ranger's unbelievable orders for us to leave, Nick and I were invited to the Kanagawa Prefectural Tournament in September, one of the most prestigious in the Japanese fight calendar. This was an open weight tournament (meaning no weight divisions) run by Yukio Nishida, who ended up starting the first Kyokushin breakaway group with Kenji Midori years later. There were 64 competitors, and I had five fights in one day. Open weight division tournaments are interesting, in that anyone of any weight can be matched up. It's not uncommon for a 155-pound (70 kg) fighter to be fighting a 220-pound (100 kg) fighter.

Wada Sensei, my hero, was there as a teacher, and had brought one of his best students to fight. How surreal can the world be? My first match was with my former hero's student in the very first round. Believe it or not, Wada's student was the hardest fight I encountered in the whole tournament. The fight went for one round, and then the maximum of two extensions – meaning two more rounds (all two minutes each). The fight was a highly skilled match with lots of high head kicks that could easily have taken either of us down. Being Wada Sensei's student, and Wada being such an incredible kicker and technician, you could see it had rubbed off on his best student.

We fought to the best of our ability, but as the rounds progressed we started to fatigue, so the fight changed from high head kicks to a war of attrition involving chest punches and thigh kicks. My opponent was a rock and showed a lot of spirit, but by the last round I could see cracks in his mask of resilience. I dug deep and really poured it on and fought hard, barraging him with a flurry of punches and inside leg kicks with all of my strength and weight behind them. With 30 seconds to go, I sensed weakness and stepped up my intensity even more. If he didn't go down soon, I thought I was going to gas out. Sure enough, he cracked and fell back, and I literally punched him off the mat. The referee pulled him back into the center, and I could hear Nick – but, incredibly, also The Ranger, of all people – in my corner yelling, "Good work, good work, go forward, punch him out again!"

This encouragement really pumped me up, and through my corner it gave me that extra edge. As a full-contact karate fighter, when you see your opponent start to weaken you really feed off that. The cracks that appear in their armor only strengthen your resolve, and when this starts to happen, it becomes game over very quickly. It's like water rushing to break through a tiny hole in a dam. That's why there is always so much emphasis placed by the Japanese on the stony-eyed and blank expression that fighters must have, and some are experts at it. Without that emotionless look, if you show any pain or weakness, you are lost from the very beginning.

I won all five of my fights convincingly in this tournament, reaching the final against Ko Tanigawa, Nishida Shihan's student who later became the Shin Kyokushin World Lightweight Champion.

I was pumped at the final. I knew I had done all the right training, and I sure wasn't coming this far to lose it now. I walked onto the mat feeling confident. I had landed some good head kicks to my earlier opponents but hadn't registered a knockout yet.

At the start of the first round I sized Tanigawa up, then moved forward aggressively when I had a game plan, because I wanted to knock him out. He struck first with some good shots, but his blows didn't hurt me; I wasn't flustered one bit, and that's when I knew the fight was mine to win.

I drove a *mawashi geri* (roundhouse kick) into his body, which made him buckle to the side. Instinctively seeing that opening, I quickly followed with a vicious descending axe kick down towards his head. My heel landed flush on top on his head, driving him into the ground and knocking him down. He wasn't unconscious, but couldn't continue.

My corner erupted in cheers, but I remember there was a funeral-like silence from the crowd, since Tanigawa was from Kanigawa so he was a crowd favorite. I didn't care – I was ecstatic that I'd knocked out such a great fighter within the first 30 seconds to win the final. But there was no jumping up and down or celebrating for me. The Kyokushin and Budo way dictates that you stand proudly and bow to the referee and your opponent, then shake his hand and give him a hug of encouragement, showing the ultimate respect.

Having fought and won the Kanagawa Tournament, I remember my idol, Wada Sensei, coming up to me afterward and congratulating me. I felt great, and he was obviously very proud of me.

This was the high point of my career. All of my *Senpais* congratulated me, and there were always sayonara parties after the tournaments where all the officials came over and congratulated me. Even The Ranger, my mortal enemy, was full of praise. You could clearly see his attitude had changed, and he never bothered Nick or me again after this.

Sosai wasn't at this tournament, but he'd heard I won, so when we got back to the dorm he was absolutely effusive with congratulations on my victory. That night he ordered in tons of pizza and cake to the *Honbu* for all of us *uchi deshi* in celebration.

After such a huge day with the tournament, the sayonara party, celebrations and the massive feed back at the dormitory, we finally returned to our sleeping quarters. By this stage, Ligo was back to the USA and Nick had taken his place on the futon next to me. Nick and I lay down on our futons and started talking, and Nick began to get emotional and said, "Judd, I don't want to take anything away from your win. I'm so happy you fought hard and won this tournament, but I was very disappointed in myself and I don't understand what I am doing wrong." He was looking at his shins, which were all busted up, and asking, "Why couldn't I win? Why did I lose? What's wrong with me?" and he broke down and started sobbing.

Remembering what Sosai often told us, "Always be hard on yourself... but kind to others," I stopped Nick in his tracks and consoled him. I said, "Listen, Nick, you're only in your second year, and this is only your first tournament. Mate, I guarantee one day you will be a champion, and next tournament I'm sure you will do much better. One day your time will come. Just keep training hard and persevere. You've got all the attributes there. Don't take this too hard, and treat it as a learning experience."

But I also told him that feeling bad and down can be a good thing. It shows that you feel bad about losing, and means that you want and need to win. This was only his first tournament, and I remember thinking that him taking this so hard – even though he was just a second-year fighting in his first big regional Japanese tournament – meant he would one day be a World Champion in his own right. Anyone who had these sort of incredibly high expectations, right from the very start of their career, was surely destined to stand on top of the dais one day.

The following morning at *chore*, Sosai made a huge

announcement about what I had achieved and loudly congratulated me. I remember as soon as he sighted me in the morning, he strode over to me in front of everyone, shook my hand, slapped me on both shoulders and said, "Wonderful, Judd. Congratulations and well done."

My dreams had come true. I was one of Sosai Oyama's Young Lions, I was a full-time teacher at the *Honbu,* and I'd just won my first major regional tournament. I truly felt like the King of the World.

CHAPTER 46
NICK'S TURN

若獅子

"Each of us has his cowardice. Each of us is afraid to lose, afraid to die. But hanging back is the way to remain a coward for life. The Way to find courage is to seek it on the field of conflict. And the sure way to victory is willingness to risk one's own life." –Sosai Oyama

Two months after the Kanagawa Tournament, Nick and I were both invited to fight in the Shizuoka Tournament, which was Branch Chief Oishi Daigo's event. We'd proven ourselves to be a threat to the Japanese fighters, since we always put on a good show and did our best without being intimidated, drawing admiration from the crowd, if not their nationalist-swayed cheers. I still had injuries from the last tournament, particularly on my shins, which were knotted and bumpy, and my right hand, which was still a deep purple color with the thumb askew, popped out of joint. It usually took about three weeks to heal properly after a tournament, so I just would work around those injuries; this was something that was expected of tournament fighters. Even with a broken thumb or cracked ribs, I'd just suck it up and keep training.

Nick and I trained very hard for this next one. We did lots of cardio, hill sprints, push-ups, sit-ups, and jumping squats. We also did a lot of heavy bag work in the basement. I really liked the basement because it was much cooler than upstairs, and always had a dirty, grungy feel about it. The bags were clean, but the weights were rusty, and there was always that smell of sweat. It really felt like a Rocky Balboa type of gym. It was always cooler in the summer, and dead silent except for the sound of work. The hard tile floor was worn and cracked; there was no glamour, no shiny mats, cushy carpets or music blasting down there like you'll find in gyms these days. It was about training long and training hard, and then training some more. Many times I'd be in the basement by myself for hours, just smashing away at the heavy bag.

I liked this style of solitary training, and I like the mental side of being able to push myself without anyone's help. I always see people with headphones on when training and I think, "Why do people need this type of thing to pump themselves up?" You should have that motivation drilled into you already, shouldn't you? Even on the days of tournaments, when I see people with headphones on, my thoughts are always: "These people are gone." I've got to say, I never saw the Japanese legends from my time (1990 to 1995) such as Matsui, Midori, Masuda, Yamaki, Kurosawa, or Kazumi with headphones on, so maybe they felt the same way.

The Shizuoka Prefectural Tournament was in November, and this was another big one, with 64 competitors and an open weight format again. Nick and I had trained harder than ever, and were becoming very strong *uchi deshi,* so we were ready and eager to fight.

I fought Ko Tanigawa in the semifinal, but lost due to a warning for grabbing. It was a frustrating fight for me, as Tanigawa would move around a lot, not letting me settle in and square off on him. He would hit me and then quickly back off or move to the side, creating angles and proving a hard target to hit. While this hit and run strategy is prevalent in boxing, it's uncommon in Kyokushin Karate, where the judges love to see fighters toe to toe, giving it their best without ever retreating or "dancing." So I grew impatient at his tactics during this fight, and tried to close in on him, inadvertently grabbing his *gi* several times and drawing fouls, which eventually led to my loss. It was a terrible way to lose and I realized that my aggressiveness and inexperience had played right into his hands.

Tanigawa was the opponent I'd beaten to win the last

tournament, so I guess he got me back. What was amazing, though, was Nick's performance. In the final, Nick knocked out Tanigawa with an axe kick after about 30 seconds, almost exactly repeating what I had done in the previous tournament. A good half-dozen of us were in Nick's corner, along with The Ranger yet again. Nick was ecstatic about his win and graciously thanked everyone for their support. I was rapt for him, finally seeing him achieve the great things I always believed he was destined for.

We had now both officially made it. At this stage, you could really say we were Sosai Oyama's boys. We had now proved ourselves as a force to be reckoned with. By this stage, both Nick and I were teaching at the *Honbu,* and I was one of the head instructors teaching at least one class a day. Often Sosai would call up Nick and I when he had guests in his office above the dojo, and he would ask us to recite the *dojo kun* to show that we were his boys and on the right track.

Knowing that I made Sosai, my teacher, master and father figure, proud was more important to me than all of the medals, trophies, and championships in the world.

CHAPTER 47
DINNERS WITH SOSAI

若獅子

Dinners with Sosai on Saturdays were always with all the *uchi deshi*, including those who were living with us only for a short time, and could vary in numbers from 10 to 20, depending on the time of the year. Dinner was always served out in huge amounts, and Sosai would always encourage us to eat huge portions. His words were: *"Takusan tabete yo. Tsuyoku nare yo* – Eat a lot, and you'll become big and strong." He would often repeat this three or four times during the meal. We would always say *osu!* Never would we ever even consider refusing another bowl of meat, vegetables, or rice. He would often test us by asking *"Onaka ippai desuka? Daijobudesuka?* – Are your stomachs full, are you okay?" To which we would always reply, *"Osu daijobu desu* – yes I'm okay; I can eat more." We'd then refill our bowls and start chowing down again, even though our stomachs felt like if we put in one more spoonful they might burst. I look back on this and realize it wasn't just an eating frenzy, but also a test.

The Saturday night meals started promptly at 6:30, and usually went for an hour to an hour and a half. Toward the end of the meal, the eating frenzy would slow down and Sosai would order one or two of the *uchi deshi* to bring out the dessert. It consisted of a lot of assorted cakes, and large pieces of watermelon – which I remember were the hardest to keep down, because they would bloat you so much. At this stage, Sosai would begin to talk about some of his old experiences and explain the life lessons he learned from them. This was by far my favorite time. I treasured it and looked forward to it every week. It meant we *uchi deshi* were up close and personal with

Sosai, and to spend any quality time with him was priceless, as his general aura was magical. And I knew the stories that would come at these mealtimes would be heard only by us *uchi deshi*.

By 1991 and 1992, he would say to Nick and I often during these meal times that we were training hard and doing well, and even things along the lines of, "One day you guys will be World Champions." I felt very proud that he would say this, but I also remember feeling a little sorry for the Japanese students, who didn't always get nearly as much praise. I can only think that because we were foreigners there, he felt we needed that extra encouragement – and you have to remember that Sosai Oyama himself was Korean, and had felt discrimination and hardship in his early days. Perhaps he wanted to ensure that we didn't have as hard a time as he did.

Sosai's stories often were about things that had happened many decades before, and he would regale us with tales of mortal fights, epic adventures, and inhuman hardships. He often said that the two worst things in life were to be hungry or lonely. I think he was referring to his time training in the mountains, and perhaps that's why he encouraged us to eat so much and to support each other like a family. No one would be hungry – or alone – as long as they were under Sosai Oyama's care.

One famous fight story I remember he related a few times. It involved a time when he was attacked by a number of bad guys with knives and other weapons. I'm not sure who they were – maybe mafia – but those were some rough, lawless times in Tokyo. I always remember that he had these incredible scars on his forearms, and he had these club-like fists, and at the time I wondered whether these were the results of those earlier battles. The stories were based in the early 1950s in Tokyo, and involved fights with the Japanese *yakuza* and the U.S. Marines who occupied Japan at the time. No matter how outnumbered he was, or what the odds, he always stood up for himself – and for others. Sosai detested those who preyed on the weak and defenseless, and many times came to the aid of someone on the

Dinners with Sosai

street that was being bullied. Though we thirsted for more details, Sosai never went into specifics; he was not one to shine on about his own merits or victories, but wanted to impress a valuable life lesson upon us. He always cheered on the underdog. This was a recurring theme in his stories and he would say, in these situations, we should be like him and always stand up for ourselves and others in need of help. He would point out that these were different times – the 1950s, after much of Japan had been demolished by Allied wartime bombing, and the country was just starting to rebuild from the rubble – but the principles could easily be applied to any time.

He would say, "Always stand up for yourself, don't take any shit, and make the bad guys pay." There was a myth, particularly in martial arts these days, that karate is a sport for promoting fitness and self-defense and confidence, and it should never to be used in the street, even if you are being attacked. It is said that you should walk away, and perhaps even take a verbal or physical beating. But if you think about this, it's really quite ridiculous. Martial arts are all about fighting. They're about training to be able to fight, not just in tournaments, but to defend yourself on the street, if need be. This doesn't mean you are to become a bully, but if you find yourself cornered and in imminent danger of physical harm, being a trained *karateka* gives you the opportunity to fight off your attackers and escape without being harmed yourself.

Sosai Oyama would often say to us *uchi deshi*, "*Nande karate yaru no?*" We wouldn't answer, as we knew the question was rhetorical, to which he would then answer: "*Kenka no tame ni tsuyoke nare kara.*" The rough translation of this question and answer being: "Why are you doing karate? So you can be strong and defend yourself in a street fight."

Even though karate and karate training in those days involved all manner of physical preparation and trials, including basics, bag work, *kata*, sparring, weights, and the incredible summer and winter camps where we would run through the ocean and stand under waterfalls, Sosai was always

235

consistent about one thing. He told us, "You are training karate to become strong fighters." This was his mantra, the thing he drilled into us time and time and time again. He said that especially because we were young, this was the time to push ourselves to our absolute limits, and focus on being the best and strongest fighters we could be.

He said that if you stick to this path, are disciplined, and persevere and train as hard as you can, then through karate and the discipline that comes with it, you will develop your strength and character, and everything else in life will follow – wealth, girlfriends, opportunities, and luxuries in life. He always encouraged us not to do go down the path of greed and doing things for money's sake, but to live virtuous lives. What was important was to train hard and give it your all. The rest would come later. Only by mastering ourselves could we be ready to master our lives, and then the world. Later on, after you had achieved everything you possibly could, then you could reflect and philosophize about the meaning of it all, and give back by training and readying the next generation. Now was not the time for that. We were young and strong, and now was the time to train hard, stay on this path and become champions.

Sosai always said it didn't matter how good your technique was; it would improve with training. It was all about your perseverance and a never give up attitude – that same fire in your belly that he'd identified in me as a skinny 17-year-old kid from Australia. Sosai always said, *"Yareba dekiru* – Try and you can do it," and *"Kare wa kami sama janai yo. Kare mo ningen dayo. Kare mo tsukarechau yo.* – Your opponent is not a God. He is human too. He bleeds and hurts just like you, and gets tired as well."

Understanding this lesson, it was just a battle of wills, and whoever wanted it more would win. More often than not, I made sure that was me.

Sosai had living quarters above his office, which he lived in during the old days, but by the time I arrived he had moved to a large, beautiful old home in one the of better parts of Tokyo. He

Dinners with Sosai

was driven around in a nice old black car, usually reserved for company presidents and the like, and he had his own full-time driver who was a current *uchi deshi* – usually nominated from either the second- or third-year students. When we were second-years, we would rotate and take shifts to guard his house.

There would be the driver and me, and we had sleeping quarters where we would stay. Our duties were to look over everything, watch out for him since he was a famous man, and open and close the doors for him (both on the house and the cars), and really act like his mini security team or bodyguards.

One time, Sosai and I drove to a shop in the winter, and he playfully threw his gloves to me when we got out of his car. I managed to catch one, but missed the second, which hit the ground before I quickly scooped it up. Sosai smiled and said, "Mmmm… you should've caught that one, too." Although he was just good naturedly teasing, to be honest I was disappointed in myself, thinking, "Judd, you played cricket for all those years, why couldn't you catch both?" If Mr. Miyagi could catch a fly between two chopsticks, then surely I could catch a pair of gloves with both hands!

To me, any failure in Sosai's eyes, no matter how small it may have seemed, was unacceptable. That was the standard he expected of us, as well as himself, and only by striving for that could we achieve greatness and honor his vision. I remember every morning when Sosai left his home and we drove him to the dojo, his wife, tall, always elegant and full of grace, would kneel on her knees to see him off, which was the Japanese tradition. It wasn't demeaning or about being subservient, but paying tribute, and Sosai's whole life was about helping and serving others, too. Sosai and his wife had met in 1945 after she had been a Tokyo beauty queen, and they were married two years later. Together had three daughters, and Sosai was definitely a family man, a great husband and father.

His 1,000-day *uchi deshi* program produced Young Lions who were world-class fighters, but the training was really about more than that. Just like he had experienced a spiritual epiphany as he trained in solitude on the mountain, we, too, had to push past our human limits. We learned the value of persevering no matter what the obstacles or odds, and only then could we prevail. Just like in life, you can always push yourself harder and keep fighting if you only believe in yourself. And that was the real reward – the feeling of contentment and spiritual bliss that comes when you have given your all…and then some.

Sosai Oyama had amassed fame, wealth, trophies, and all of the physical trappings you could hope for in a lifetime. But deep down, his life's work was to help others achieve that same spiritual bliss through physical mastery, though it was a sword that could be sharpened through discipline, perseverance, and overcoming hardship. He could have easily retired or rested on his laurels, but even in his 70s, he was more disciplined and devoted than ever. I found out that Sosai hosted huge karate tournaments every four years, spending two to three million dollars of his own money to bring in 255 of the best fighters to compete, just to share what he loved and believed in, and to help others.

Like the Kyokushin mantra says, "Keep your head bowed low but eyes gazed towards the sky. Be reserved in speech but with an indomitable fighting spirit and generous in heart. This is the Kyokushin spirit."

Sosai Oyama wasn't just training us for karate, but preparing us to live good and noble lives. By doing so, we'd be able to help many others live good lives, too. That is why he still spent every day working at the dojo, why he dedicated his life to producing men of great character who could aid society, and why he'd taken a chance on a young Australian kid who couldn't come up with the entire amount for his *uchi deshi* program, but had a fire in his belly and was dedicated to one day roar like a Young Lion.

CHAPTER 48
GETTING IN TROUBLE

若獅子

"In the martial arts, introspection begets wisdom. Always see contemplation on your actions as an opportunity to improve."
—*Sosai Oyama*

In the second half of my third year, Pettas, the Pink Panther and I met an Israeli guy who started training at the school named Avri. Nick and I soon became friends with him. He seemed like a pretty easygoing guy. One day he asked us if we wanted to make some extra money selling jewelry twice a week for a few hours. We said, "Sure, why not? As long as it's outside of class times."

Avri and his partner Benny ran these jewelry street stalls, where they sold cheap silver jewelry and an array of knockoffs, including Louis Vuitton bags and watches. Everything was made in Korea for five to 10 dollars and sold for $300 in bubble time Japan with its roaring economy. So, two days a week for two hours at a time, on Monday and Wednesday, we stood at the booths and they paid us 10,000 yen (about $100 USD) each time. They made millions, and we made peanuts, but it was great money to us at the time, especially with no other form of income as *uchi deshi*.

Looking back, they wanted us to appear as muscle against the opposing Israelis trying to take their spots. I guess it worked, because we never had any problems with the other Israelis. They did this for about two years, and although Nick and I only worked there for two months, it lead to consequences that almost got me kicked out of the *uchi deshi* program.

I walked downstairs one morning after the *chore*, and as I

walked into the foyer these two Japanese men in suits asked me if I was Judd Reid. When they produced badges, I knew exactly what it was about. They wanted to take me to the police station immediately, but I asked if I could go and change my clothes first in the dorm, and they said okay. Robo San was there, as they followed me to the dorm, and words were exchanged between them. Robo looked less than impressed. I was, basically, under arrest.

I remember walking into the dorm and changing into jeans, and I saw Nick sitting there. Word had obviously got around because I said, "Mate, I'm screwed. Do you know what's going on?" He said, "Yes, I do." I said, "Can I borrow your belt to hold up my pants?" and I remember him refusing to give it to me. Although it may seem a small thing, since I was taking the rap for all of us, I remember that really hurt me.

When I got to the police station, part of the interview was to show me months of surveillance pictures of the street stalls. I remember the police flipping through the photos of me standing in front of a stall, selling fake watches and bags, and asking, "That's you right?" to which I'd acknowledge that it was. Then another photo of me, asking, "Again you, right?" and I again I'd answer yes. Then came a picture of Nick, and once again they said, "You, right?" and without hesitation I said yes, realizing it was a golden opportunity to keep my mate out of trouble. I think I may have told Nick about this at some later stage, but I hope he appreciates what I did for him that day. They never even got any photos of the Pink Panther, which was typical for his brazen personality and charmed life.

I was being dragged in every day for further interviews and investigation and questioning. They made me sit at a big table, with several officers facing me and barraging me with questions, over and over. I wasn't handcuffed, but I couldn't leave, and even had to ask permission for a bathroom break. This went on for five days in a row. At the end of it all, the guy who interviewed me actually liked me, and asked me, "Don't you know that selling knockoffs is wrong?" Although I knew it

Getting in Trouble

was wrong, as a young kid you don't always fully think things through, so I said I knew it was, but I never knew exactly how serious it was. To be honest, I really didn't think about what I was doing, or whether it was actually illegal. I knew it was wrong, but I thought the police were okay with this hustle, if that makes sense. It doesn't, really, but I was still a kid who knew very little outside of karate back then.

On day two, when I came from back from the police station, Sosai called me up to his office, along with Minami *Senpai* – the most senior teacher at the *Honbu*, under Sosai. He was scowling, and he looked at me in a way I'd never seen him look at me before. He gave me a massive dressing down, his eyes never wavering from looking at me directly, and his mannerisms and body language made it clear he was disappointed in me. He asked me to write him a letter explaining why I was in Japan, and why I wanted to be an *uchi deshi*. At the same time, he turned to Minami and scolded him, saying he should have had more control over the *uchi deshi* and what they were doing.

Holding superiors 100% accountable for those under them was the norm in Japanese society, and I remember one time at one of the summer camps when a few of us got caught sneaking out to go to an ice cream parlor without permission, Minami ripped into the Pink Panther for not watching us, and ordered him to do jumping squats all night. So Sosai actually scolded Minami worse than me when I got arrested, and I felt bad about this. He said, "I can't blame Judd for doing this and getting out in the world," but I knew it was all my fault. I heard when I returned the first day about 6 PM that Sosai had been calling the police station every 30 minutes to find out what was going on.

So, with the help of the Japanese, I wrote a long, in-depth letter about my intentions, how much I loved and was honored to be Sosai's *uchi deshi*, about how this was my only dream in life, and promising that nothing like this would ever happen again. The letter ran to about three pages, and I meant every word.

I gave Sosai the letter the next day, and nothing more was

ever said. I guess he accepted what I had to say and assumed that I'd had enough of a shock without prolonging the agony. To this day, I wonder why he didn't kick me out, but I am so appreciative that he was so forgiving, because it would have changed my life forever.

I was interviewed by the cops for a whole week before they finally said to me, "That's it, all is okay, you can go now." I heard later on that this was all due to Sosai's recommendations and pleadings. You have to remember that he had incredible fame, influence, respect, and power in Japanese society, and this was likely the only thing that saved me. To give you an idea of what could have happened: at least 10 to 15 other workers, as well as the two Israeli owners all got the same sentence. The poor people all did about six months jail time for their illegal activities. This was mostly due to pressure from Louis Vuitton, which in those days had its own personal police force and investigation unit that traveled around the world, forcing the local authorities to enforce copyright laws. It probably seemed like a holiday for Avri and Benny, who had undoubtedly stashed away millions over the two years, but imagine all the part-time workers who made a meager living from manning the stalls, all having to do the same amount of time.

For me, letting Sosai down was worse than having to do jail time. My biggest disappointment in my life thus far was putting Sosai in an awkward situation where he had to clean up my mess, and I swore to myself I would learn from that mistake and never do something like that again that would jeopardize our relationship.

CHAPTER 49
BROTHERS IN ARMS

若獅子

"Always remember that the true meaning of Budo is that soft overcomes hard, small overcomes large." –Sosai Oyama

It's interesting to look back at some of the characters the *Honbu* attracted.

Big Dave started coming to the *Honbu* classes in 1992. He was a massive, smiling guy with a great nature, and although not from a Kyokushin background, we all liked him and welcomed him into our ranks. He was a 6'4", 265-pound (120 kg) monster that could bench press 485 pounds (220 kg) and squat 600 pounds (275 kg). He had been a star footballer at the University of Miami until both his knees blew out, and now he was in Japan working for a number of different businesses.

He was always smiling, positive, and had a great attitude – kind of like a monstrous, superhumanly strong teddy bear. Big Dave really was larger than life. He used to laugh about the fact that the other students liked him to come in just to use him as a big punching bag. But you just knew nothing was ever going to hurt Big Dave, who could shrug off punches and kicks that would drop other students like he was shooing away flies.

Big Dave went on to become a very successful businessman, importing goods between Japan and America – anything from sushi to bulk containers of clothing.

Nick, my best mate, went on to become a professional K-1 Kickboxing star and a huge Japanese television personality. Years later I would be watching TV in Thailand and there was Nick on the telly, a celebrity host for one of the Japan's biggest

TV shows! He carved out a niche for himself in Japan that would only be possible for very few people.

The Pink Panther became a colorful figure in Tokyo, president of dozens of companies and very successful, though he came to live with one foot in the shadowy underworld of the *yakuza*. He was always going to be different and do things his own way. He was always going to be the Pink Panther. No matter what, however, we will always be brothers for life.

Kuruda was the perfect *uchi deshi,* and a great fighter as well. You knew he was going to stay in Kyokushin, and he eventually became a branch chief under Matsui's group. He got to the best eight in an All Japan, and is well respected in the Kyokushin community.

Kato stayed in Kyokushin, too, running his own karate school as well as opening a small restaurant.

Ishiguro *Senpai,* who was two years my senior and was always pretty nice to us first-years, is now a branch chief of Matsui's organization and runs his own dojo in Shizuoka.

Of course, there were also those many part-time *uchi deshi* and *soto deshi* who trained with us during this period, and some of them I consider brothers as well.

I remember Ronin Katz fondly, a kind and friendly man from Israel that often trained in the *Honbu* during my time as an *uchi deshi*. He was a higher grade than me, but would often take Nick and I out for dinner when we were second- and third-years. Of course we didn't have a dime (nor yen) to our names, so Ronin always gladly volunteered to pay the bill. We always appreciated his generosity, and enjoyed laughing and joking in his company. Of course I appreciated it then, but looking back, those small acts of kindness have meant the world, and I am happy to still be in close contact with Ronin and lifelong friends.

Kyokushin has a way of bonding people like no other sport, and you just knew that our paths were destined to cross time and again over the years.

We as *uchi deshi* were brothers in arms. We always backed one another against outsiders. We were encouraged to smash each other in class, but if outsiders came in and tried to bully the *uchi deshi,* we stuck together. Now and then, foreigners who came over to train would try to prove themselves against the *uchi deshi.*

One time in particular there was a higher-grade foreigner who was really hurting one of my brothers, bashing the younger and mismatched *uchi deshi* without letting up at all. When it was my turn to fight him, it was time to settle the score and defend our *uchi deshi.*

When the sparring started, I went hard at him from the get-go. He was strong, too, but it didn't matter, as there was no time limit to this fight – it would go until one of us dropped, and that sure wasn't going to be me. We exchanged vicious bone-rattling blows for about three minutes straight. I didn't know his name or where he was from, but I was upset that he'd intentionally hurt a younger student, and was there to return the punishment – and he knew it. Soon, he started to buckle. I could have easily kicked him in the head and finished it, but I chose to hammer his body instead, inflicting more justice. Finally, I dropped him with a roundhouse kick to his battered ribs. The other *uchi deshi* thanked me with their eyes, but we didn't have to say a word.

There were many karate superstars who came into the dojo to train, but the vast majority of them were honorable, respectful, and just there to train hard. There's no way I can name them all. Of course, Matsui was Sosai's number one man, and I often encountered many of the top Japanese fighters of the time. But let me tell you about one of them that really left an impression.

His name was Hajime Kazumi, and he was a legend in the sport and a fighter with incredible heart. I remember Kazumi at a demonstration Sosai had us doing in front of some very important people. Kazumi had just placed second at the All Japan in 1992, beating all these Kyokushin legends along the way, only to lose in the final. The guy was a freak, only 22 years old at the time, but a new breed of fighting machine that would end up first or second in the All Japan or World Tournaments for 10 straight years in a row. No one else has ever done this.

So, we were at this demonstration, and he was the most humble, quiet guy. There was something very special about him, which I'd never seen before. Nick and I were doing a *kata* demonstration. Kazumi was going to do a baseball bat breaking demonstration, and Matsui asked, "How many bats are you going to break?" Kazumi humbly answered, "Just one. I've never broken a baseball bat before." Matsui started laughing and said, "You could break a buffalo's legs with your power. You're going to break four baseball bats."

Kazumi just said, "*osu,*" and carried on stretching, not even flinching at Matsui's order. So they wrapped these four baseball bats up tight. Nick and I went out first and did our demo, and then a few more demos were done, like ice breaks with *shoto,* or the blade of the hand. Kazumi then came out and lined up these baseball bats, which were being held tightly in place by other students. He let out a big loud *kiai* and unleashed an almighty kick, smashing the bats into splinters and sawdust like it was nothing. Everybody clapped and cheered. Kazumi bowed to Sosai, the officials, and the people attending. In my head, I remember thinking, "This is the new breed. He is going to dominate for years to come."

Kazumi is such a nice guy, each time I meet him. He represents the true warrior and Budo way of a martial artist, and he's just a great guy. He's humble, reserved in speech, a super nice guy, and has a huge fighting spirit like a samurai.

We were far more than just a bunch of individuals plucked from their daily lives and deposited together to work, sweat, and struggle together in a Japanese dormitory. The hardships we went through bonded us forever. We stuck together like a loyal and protective tribe. I chose the way of a *budo karateka* well before I became an *uchi deshi*, but my time as a Young Lion branded that decision into my spirit forever.

CHAPTER 50
100-MAN KUMITE, FIGHTS 91 THROUGH 99

若獅子

After I'd fought 90 black belts in a row, I was in another world. It was all a blur, and it seemed like I was out of my body, watching two other fighters battle it out. Even walking back to my corner between fights was now too much of an effort, so I stood in one place and just kept punching on. Anton and the boys yelled, "Judd, you're almost there! Only 10 fights to go."

I tilted my head back, gazing up towards the sky. My mind wasn't working right, but I wasn't going to let everyone down. I was fighting for my family, friends, and to honor Sosai Oyama, just as much as I was fighting for myself.

It was my last stand. Right there, in the bottom floor dojo of an Osaka arena, in front of all of my family, friends, judges and officials, I decided to fight like a Young Lion, even though opponent after opponent had cracked my ribs, smashed into stomach, chest and thighs, and bruised my organs so badly that I'd urinate nothing but blood for a week afterwards.

With that last stretch of fighters, I gave it all I had. I'm proud to say that I actually punched on and took it to the final few fighters, giving every ounce of spirit I had left, slugging it out in a dream-like state.

Again and again, I let out an almighty *kiai* and dragged myself back out. The referee said something to me, but it didn't register. My opponent moved in. I couldn't see faces anymore, just white *gi* with black belts. He must have hit me, but I didn't feel anything. I swayed and stumbled, but refused to take a step back, refusing to give up. Punch, punch, punch. I did not stop until the ref yelled *Yame!* - Stop! - and pulled us apart.

Ninety-nine fights down.

The walls were closing in a little tighter. I had one more fight to go.

CHAPTER 51
GRADUATION

若獅子

"A man who understands decorum and the courtesies is a great treasure; I hope to train and send into society as many such men as I can." –Sosai Oyama

I graduated from the Kyokushin Karate 1,000-day Young Lions *uchi deshi* program on March 15, 1993. Although I was obviously not the first or only foreigner who trained at the *Honbu*, I was the first to successfully complete and graduate after 1,000 days of training in Sosai Masutatsu Oyama's Young Lions program. This was the proudest day of my life, and still is even now. My dreams at graduation had been fulfilled. I was happy, relieved, and proud. Proud, especially, because many people were counting on me – including Sosai, all my mates back in the dojo in Australia (many of whom had helped me get to Japan in the first place), and my mum and Rizza, who had worked so hard and sacrificed so much so I could chase my dream. I went on to fight in many World Karate Championships and achieved many of the goals I set out to achieve, but none compare to the feelings I felt having completed this course.

We stood at attention, just like we did at the start of every class, but this time we were all sharply dressed in suits and ties. Sosai stood at the front of the dojo and addressed us in his booming voice, congratulating us all for giving an outstanding effort. He told us that this was only the beginning, and he'd still expect a lot from us from here on out. Sosai then announced each of our names and presented each of us individually with a graduation certificate and plaque, shaking our hands and offering his encouragement.

THE YOUNG LIONS

At graduation there were eight of us, in the largest graduating class I had ever heard of. There was the Pink Panther (Yamakagi), Kuruda, Ishida, Kumokai, Kato, Suzuki, Oshikiri, and me. These guys were all different people, with distinct personalities, but all incredibly tough individuals, and somehow we'd all made it through the toughest karate course in the world. During our three years of training we forged a bond of brotherhood that would last forever, surviving wave after wave of superhuman physical and mental testing. At the end, I was closest to the Pink Panther, Kato, Kuruda, and of course Nick, who was a year below me. This was the high point of my life, I thought, as I looked around our dorm room as we all got ready to go out an *izakaya* restaurant that night to celebrate, taking in the smiles, laughter, and back slaps of congratulations.

Of course were known as Kyokushin *Honbu uchi deshi,* but Sosai Oyama also had a name for his dormitory where the *uchi deshi* lived, and that was called *Wakajishi Ryo,* which in English means the Young Lions Dormitory. When I'd tell Japanese people I met that I lived in a *Wakajishi Ryo,* they always looked at me with a puzzled expression (especially the girls), trying to make sense of a foreigner who was a Young Lion. Those who could speak English would ask, "Young Lions Dormitory?" Even to the Japanese, this was a bit of an unusual Japanese phase. But I could see they liked it, and most of them responded with an impressed, "*sugoi,*" or "that's great!" It had strength about it. Sosai had a plan for us, all right. Really, Young Lions is exactly what we were, and there was even a symbol and picture of two lions on our graduation certificates.

I'm sure Sosai Oyama pictured himself as a Young Lion in his early days, too. Look at what he had been through: In his twenties, just after World War II; Korean-born, he would have had a hard time in Japan, no doubt. I'm sure every day would have been a battle, and he fought his way through. What an incredible man. Even in his late 60s, every day he had the same commitment and drive, turning up to the dojo early and driving

Graduation

passion into us to excel and give it our best. He had been doing this his whole life.

Sosai was the best leader I've ever come across, building an organization with over 10 million members loyal to the best spirit of Kyokushin Karate. Along the way, he wrote dozens of books about martial arts, for both children and adults. He even produced movies, including one called *The Strongest Karate* that became pretty famous. He had dojos throughout Japan with millions of students. He also had dojos in nearly every country in the world, and he hosted yearly camps in Japan for the top dojo operators to come and train. It was also an opportunity for Sosai to take a good look at the men and women he charged with spreading his teachings, since it was so important to him to maintain the highest standards of Kyokushin.

Sosai Oyama travelled the world at his own expense, talking, teaching, and hosting seminars to spread his martial arts philosophies.

Sosai said that life starts at graduation; so now it was our job to go out and teach. I knew that I had a lot of work to do if I was going to achieve my goal of becoming World Champion. I wasn't even thinking about the 100-man *kumite* – especially after watching Masuda in 1991. But I wanted to fight in the world championships and one day become World Champion.

A couple of days after graduation, Sosai took us out on the town to celebrate. It was the happiest moment of my life. The seniors were all there, alongside Sosai, to congratulate us, and now we were one of them. Sosai had arranged a huge dinner in honor of our graduation, and it was a grand occasion. Sosai's wife was also present. The dinner was in a big *izakaya*, a traditional Japanese style restaurant, and Sosai arranged a massive feast with unlimited beer for us. He wanted us to really let loose, and we all yelled out *kampai* many times and chugged down the beers. We were all just so happy that we didn't want the night to end. We *uchi deshi* took turns standing up to sing, and the event was very loud and raucous.

Sosai had booked a smaller private room in the restaurant

THE YOUNG LIONS

right beside our main table, where he and Mrs. Oyama sat, and yelled out to Nick and I to join him. Sosai asked me, "Judd, what are your intentions now that you have graduated? What do you want to do?" I replied, "*Osu*, I wish to go to Sweden. The Swedish Kyokushin Organization has asked me to teach at various dojos there."

After graduating, I was really looking forward to traveling and seeing the world outside Japan. Months earlier, the Swedish Karate Organization contacted Sosai to inquire about me, as they needed his approval before offering my any position since I was his personal student. But no matter where I went or what I did, I was dedicated to making him proud.

Nick and I sat there in the smaller room with Sosai and Mrs. Oyama, eating huge amounts of gourmet beef, sushi, vegetables and rice as he looked on encouragingly. Sosai praised us for our effort over the years, and told us how proud he was. I remember that moment with Sosai, Mrs. Oyama, and Nick as the happiest and most golden time of my life, and that will stay with me forever.

Sosai Oyama used to say: "One becomes a beginner after 1,000 days of training, and an expert after 10,000 days of practice." Well, I'd completed my thousand days, and now it was time to begin practicing to become an expert.

Thank you, Sosai Oyama. You completely changed my whole life, and I'll always owe you a huge debt of gratitude for this.

CHAPTER 52
THE REAL SOSAI OYAMA

若獅子

By March of 1993, I had spent almost three years training under my idol, Sosai Oyama. He had invested a lot of time with me and the other *uchi deshi*, had proven himself a very kind man, a great teacher and public speaker, and an incredible motivator. He had this indomitable belief in what he was doing, and that just had to rub off on his students. They believed in him 100%, and he was always consistent and very fair to all.

People always ask me, "What was Sosai Oyama like?" I try to give them an accurate and short answer that sums up who he was, but I'm not good with words, so sometimes I feel I don't give his memory the justice it deserves. I mean, to me, Sosai was a surrogate father, the best one I'd ever known, and his teachings have served as my moral compass in life. But if I say that to people, they're going to look at me kind of strangely. Sosai Oyama was a complex man, with many great attributes, and it's hard to explain his character in just a few sentences.

In my life, I've had a few amazing teachers, but no one was more important to me than Sosai Masutatsu Oyama. From day one, when I arrived in the *Honbu,* Sosai was very warm and welcoming, and I felt an immediate connection. He demanded absolute discipline, effort, and concentration, but he often preached the importance of enjoying yourself in life, so soon you can laugh at the hardships and learn to love the challenges. He was a very evolved and conscious person, always focused on his overall vision of creating strong gentlemen of high character, first and foremost, so society could benefit.

His teachings transcended race, nationalities, religions, and war. Think about it – living side by side as brothers in his dorm were Israelis and Iranians, in a time when those two nations were embroiled in bloody conflict. But Sosai believed that karate was the vehicle for us to create better families, better children, better societies, and ultimately, a more peaceful world.

But he also never fully shed the garments of the underdog, even after spending almost all of his life in Japan. He had come over from Korea when he was only 13 years old, but it must have left a lasting impression on him what it felt like to be an outsider, and I can only imagine the abuse and torment he went through, as those two countries often had a checkered history.

I remember one time I was on guard duty and sitting in his car while we drove somewhere. He had a mobile phone in his car – one of the first, as the technology was brand new – and he was speaking to someone. I was confused, because I couldn't understand the words until I figured out it was Korean, the language of his birth country. No matter how far he came in life, he would never forget where he was from, and humility was one of the noblest traits he instilled in us Young Lions.

Sosai was more than just a karate teacher to me; he was a great human being as well, someone to aspire to be like. At the beginning I looked at him as a karate master with remarkable strength, who could perform incredible physical feats, but after getting to know him so well I realized he was also a deeply spiritual person with great thinking and deep philosophies about life in general. This may sound a little over the top, but when I see the Dalai Lama on TV these days, I see a lot of Sosai Oyama in him, and vice versa.

By the end of my time as an *uchi deshi,* Sosai really felt like my father. We had a deep connection, and I had built up an incredible amount of admiration and respect for him – not just as a karate teacher, but also as a person and a kind and compassionate human being. As for what he thought of me, I can't speak for him, but he always seemed to be proud of me, and I know he respected me for the loyalty and hard work it took to complete the Young Lions course. He knew I'd given up everything in Australia, and how hard that would have been to leave all my family and friends behind to come and train under him and follow the *budo* way.

Sosai Oyama was very old school. I look back at him now – with the '60s and '70s suits and hats he used to wear, the old black Toyota Crown Presidents car he used to be driven around in – and I think this signified part of his personality. His teaching philosophies were simple and straight to the point. Greatness comes only with good old-fashioned hard work. But even more than that, he was creating great people to go out into the world.

On our graduation certificate, or *Wakajishiryo* Certificate of Completion, is written: "We hereby certify that you have been enduring the severe and demanding dormitory life of a personal student of Sosai Oyama for three years, and that you have been fully devoted to our Japanese traditional karate. Therefore, we expect you will be a more advanced and devoted person, able to contribute to peace and good relationships throughout the world as a Young Lion with an indomitable Kyokushin spirit."

People always say Sosai Oyama had an aura about him. I spent three years with him, and I can attest that he emitted that positive energy that very special people have – and much, much more. He had this uncanny ability to enter a room and have everyone stop what they were doing to fix their gaze upon him. These days, they would call that charisma. Even if he were not known as the famous Sosai Mas Oyama, I'm sure within minutes of meeting a group of strangers he would become immediate friends with them and make them all feel comfortable. This was just who he was.

By the time I had completed the Young Lions course, I'm sure Sosai Oyama had big plans for my future. I was devoted to him, his philosophies of life, and his style of martial arts, and I had big dreams myself.

CHAPTER 53
100-MAN KUMITE
- MY FINAL FIGHT

若獅子

After my 99th fight, my team had to hold onto me, to keep me from falling down on the short 30-second break before my last fight. I was totally withdrawn from the world.

"Last one, Judd, last one. You can do it! You can do it!" they yelled. My heart was pounding, my body wanted to curl up in a ball and stop. But something came to me, a voice in my head that kept me going. It was Sosai's words, ringing deep through my consciousness: "*Yareba dikeru!*" (If you try, you can do it!)

But it couldn't have been Sosai yelling those words, as he wasn't there. The man that had changed my life, set me on my course to destiny, and the one I had grown to love like a father had passed away in April of 1994 at 71 years of age, only one year after I had graduated as a Young Lion. I found out with a letter slipped under my door. At the time, they said it was lung cancer. But Sosai never smoked and had been in perfect health, and I'd trained with him only a week before after returning to visit the *dojo*.

Sosai's sudden passing was a shock to all of us, especially the *uchi deshi* who had spent his last years with him, and the entire martial arts community mourned. I was shattered, but no one questioned his death or suspected foul play at the time.

"*Yareba dikeru!*"

I heard it again, but it was the guys in my corner yelling those words to me this time, somehow knowing exactly what I needed to hear to keep me going – the words my master had said all of those years earlier, stirring something in my soul.

"*Isshhhhaaaaaaaa!*" I yelled at the top of my voice. I could feel my team with me now. I could feel Sosai's presence looking down on me. I wasn't alone. I realized that I was never really alone.

I stepped out into the center of the mat.

My last fight was against Minami, a long-time rival and someone I respected deeply. After bowing gingerly to the referee, I dragged my left foot forward, trying to keep some balance. I hadn't been knocked down once by an opponent's blows in 99 fights, and I wasn't about to go down now.

Minami attacked, and I tried to block his crushing punches awkwardly, swatting with my cramped hands like I was trying to hit a mosquito. I used my *kiai* as I counterpunched, mustering every bit of fight left in me.

We punched away at each other. Minami pushed me hard – he wasn't going to give this to me on a golden platter!

Minami kept driving his punches into my smashed-up chest, my *gi* covered in sweat – and, now, blood splotches, too.

"*Yareba dikeru.Yareba dikeru!*" I heard the guys in my corner scream.

I did not stop.

The match felt like it went on forever.

Through my haze, I finally heard the referee yell, "*Yamei!*" at the top of his voice, barely audible over the screams and cheers from my corner and everyone in the audience. It was over.

I slumped down, nearly collapsing to the ground. Minami and the ref helped me back up. Minami hugged me. It was over.

I may have fought alone that day, but I represented so many.

I had done it.

I had done it! We had done it!

I dragged my feet over to the official's table and shook everyone's hand, without really knowing where I was. My girlfriend, Mo, was there to give me a big hug, and so did my beautiful mum, who was in tears, along with my sister, Alex.

My support team rushed over to do the same, and I was totally relieved it was over.

The Japanese fighters gathered around to congratulate me, picking me up and throwing me into the air again and again, yelling and cheering. It hurt me terribly, but they were so excited, and I made sure to thank and shake hands with each and every one of them.

I didn't want to sit. I wanted to stay standing. I don't know why, but I just did. Maybe because I knew I wouldn't be able to get back up. I collapsed into the loving embraces of my mum and sister, the warm cheers of my brothers Anton, Nick, Ned, Paul, and all of my supporters.

It was finally over. I had successfully completed the 100-man *kumite*.

AFTERWORD

若獅子

"I fought in many battles over my life. I won some, and lost some. But my hardest battle by far was the 100-man kumite." –Judd Reid

The next day, I was back at that same dojo in Osaka, but this time in a business suit as I watched a children's karate tournament. The kids came up to me and wanted my autograph, which was an unfamiliar thing for me, and I received congratulations and took photos with many of the other fighters and spectators in attendance. It was fun (though I tried not to let on how sore I was), but watching the children compete, I think I was more nervous for them than I'd been for my own 100-man *kumite!*

The duty of a karate fighter with experience such as mine is to continue to teach, and all I want to do from now on is pass on the knowledge I learned from Sosai and 20 years of tournament fighting.

I was invited to help teach a summer camp in Sweden in mid 2015 and found I really enjoyed it. I knew I loved teaching karate followers of all ages and levels, but I found I really loved the intense camp atmosphere, giving people a taste of my own *uchi deshi* experience on a smaller scale.

Since then, I have taught at a dozen similar camps and seminars, and soon I had so many requests from fighters all around the world that in 2016 I began my own *uchi deshi* camps right here in Jomtien, Thailand for full-contact fighters from any martial art or style.

The first few camps went spectacularly, and all of the participants gave it their all and improved so much over a short time with three-a-day workouts. I couldn't help but think of training in the *Honburi* dojo and summer camps with Sosai Oyama as we yelled "Fighto!" and ran on the beach in formation.

I'll keep hosting a number of these special *uchi deshi* camps every year, and I've even given them a fitting name: The Uchi Deshi Camp.

Of course, it hasn't all been perfect since retiring from professional fighting and completing the 100-man *kumite*. It took me a while to figure out what I wanted to do with my life, and to reaffirm my purpose.

The decades of extreme punishment on my body also took their toll, as my hip was so bad I could barely walk. But I'm happy to say that within six months of having hip replacement surgery I was training again, and soon regained my strength and flexibility almost like in my prime.

I feel confident about what the future holds. I'm in my favorite place in the world and happy in my new role as retired fighter and teacher. This will be my future, and I'm happy about that.

Since retiring, I've been living in Thailand with Mo, who was my girlfriend at the time I did the 100-man fight and is now my beautiful wife. We have a two-year-old son, Max, who looks great in his little *gi* and already runs around the house yelling "*Osu!*"

Now that I have my own boy, things are different, and I definitely enjoy a more quiet and laid-back life. All I wish is for him is to be a happy kid and live a healthy lifestyle, no matter what road he chooses. Although I have to admit that I've got him on oatmeal, avocado, and bananas every day for breakfast, trying to build him up strong and healthy – then straight into fighting. Haha only joking! Golf and tennis, that's where the money's at – and he'll never get hit!

I love that I'm able to head down to the beach with Max and Mo each afternoon. We drink a coconut juice and watch the waves lapping against the shore, or have dinner right by the beach as the sun goes down. I still work and train hard each

Afterword

day, but my favorite time is when I can go home to my family. It's a great lifestyle, and I will continue doing this for as long as I can.

I think it's not until you grow up that you realize how important family is, and how much love you have for them. My mum is my superhero more than ever, and I appreciate the job she did raising two kids by herself. It must have been tough for her, but she never complained. I realize that many people in life have great warrior spirits, even if they don't fight. My mum and Rizza have always supported me 100%. Without that support, I never would have achieved my dream of going to Japan, and my life surely would have turned out differently.

So, four years after I completed the 100-man *kumite*, what does it mean to me? If I'm honest, just thinking about it brings memories of extreme pain! All I can do is shake my head and say that it was the hardest thing I've ever done in my life. However, through all the pain, I still thought of Sosai looking down on me and smiling. More than anything, it was him in my thoughts right after the fight.

This was the pure definition of *Osu no Seishin*, persevering through the impossible and winning in the end, that Sosai had drilled into us Young Lions so many years ago. I had finally done it. I had taken on the ultimate challenge of the spirit and won.

"The best reason for learning karate is to develop character – to make a good man first and a strong man second. This must be understood in advance." –Sosai Oyama

GLOSSARY OF JAPANESE WORDS

若獅子

Karate: *Empty hand/ from the hand*

Uchi Deshi: *Live in student / personal student of Sosai Mas Oyama*

Kyokushin: *Ultimate Truth*

Kumite: *A fight or number of fights to take place*

Osu (pronounced 'Oss'): *Yes, I will endure*

Sosai: *Founder and Master of the organization*

Gambatte / Gambarre: *Fight on*

Sensei: *Teacher*

Shihan: *Master*

Senpai: *Senior*

Kohai: *Junior*

Itadakimasu: *It will be a feast*

Gochisosamadeshita: *It was a feast*

Dogi: *Karate uniform*

Obi: *Belt*

Shitsureishimashita: *Excuse me in the most polite form of Japanese*

Sumimasen: *Pardon me*

Honbu: *Headquarters for the kyokushin dojo in the world*

Taiko: *Wooden drum*

Chore: *Morning ceremony*

Ichi: *One*

Ni: *Two*

San: *Three*

Soto Deshi: *Outside student*

Yareba Dekiru: *If you try, you can do it*

Kare wa Kami sama janai yo: *Your opponent is not a God*

Kare mo ningen dayo: *He is human too*

Kaikan: *International headquarters*

Fudo Dachi: *Standing at attention*

Wakajishi: *Young Lions*

Wakajishiryo: *Young Lions dormitory*

Ryoka: *Young Lions dormitory song*

Kancho: *Director of the organization*

Kyu: *Intermediate grade*

Seishin: *Spirit*

Osu no Seishin: *Never give up!*

若獅子

Karate has been my life. I started training at 12 years of age, and Wada Sensei said that I would be Australia champion by 18. He was correct, as I won the Victoria lightweight division at 17 years old. Six months later I won the Australian lightweight division in Melbourne. It was just the start of my career, as I won the Victorian and Australian Kyokushin heavyweight division years later as well.

Throughout my fighting career I came in 2nd or 3rd place multiple times in international tournaments. It wasn't until I was 39 years old that I finally won the world heavyweight full contact karate championship.

But it wasn't until one year after that, at the age of 40, that I completed the hardest challenge of my life: the 100-man Kumite.

My pro fighting career behind me, I now host Uchi Deshi Karate Camps in beautiful Thailand.

www.ThailandKarateCamps.com

Representing Chikara Kyokushin International, I work hard every day to pass on the many lessons that Sosai Oyama taught me so many years ago. I feel it is my responsibility carry on his legacy, and I'm honored to do so.

Thank you very much for taking the time to read my story, The Young Lions.

I hope this book has inspired you and I wish you only the best on your chosen path.

Love the challenge!

Never give up!

Osu!

- Judd Reid -

Anton Cavka with Judd in Cambodia in 2015, getting some training in and working on the book.

若獅子

Anton Cavka

Anton Cavka was Judd's lifelong best friend, moving from Melbourne to live in Japan for 16 years, where he ran the biggest automobile import companies in the country. When Judd took on the 100-man fight, Anton was there with a camera to document the whole thing, from training, private interviews and footage the day of the fight, culminating in the award-winning film, 100 Man Fight. Tragically, Anton passed away in Phnom Penh, Cambodia before he could see this book completed. This book is dedicated to him.

Anton Cavka and Judd at the premier movie screening of the *100 Man Fight* film, Astor Theater in Melbourne, Australia.

若獅子

Norm Schriever

Norm Schriever is a pro blogger, best-selling author, cultural mad scientist and enemy of the comfort zone. He currently lives in Southeast Asia and sits on the Board of several charities that advocate for the rights of women and children around the world. You can find his critically acclaimed book, *The Queens of Dragon Town*, and all of his work on Amazon.com or at his site, NormWrites.com.

Anton Cavka and Norm Schriever in a tuk-tuk in Phnom Penh, Cambodia in 2015, working on *The Young Lions* book.

若獅子

若獅子

Judd's son, Max, kicking his Dad's butt at the beach in Thailand.

若獅子